Betty J. Manning

Seven Generations at Stream Cliff Farm

Great-Great Grandparents

Great Grandparents

Grandparents

Parents

Betty

Gerald

Children

Grandchildren

Heart to Heart Publishing, Inc.

Heart to Heart Publishing, Inc.
528 Mud Creek Road • Morgantown, KY 42261
(270) 526-5589
www.hearttoheartpublishinginc.com

Title:*Secrets of the Garden Path with Recipes*
ISBN: 978-1-937008-09-3
Library of Congress: 2011943596
Copyright 2011
Publication Date: March 2012

Editor: Suzanne Nevins
Senior Editor: L.J. Gill
Designer: April Yingling

1 0 9 8 7 6 5 4 3 2

Printed in China

Heart to Heart books are available at a special discount for bulk purchases for fund raising efforts, sales promotions or educational use. Author and Illustrator available for book signings. Contact Heart to Heart Publishing for more information. Fax: (270) 526-7489

Secrets of the Garden Path

with Recipes

For many years Stream Cliff Farm has been a center for herb and flower lovers. The Civil War era farm has been in the same family, including the Manning's grandchildren, for seven generations. Stream Cliff also has historical significance: it was raided during the Civil War by Morgan's Raiders.

In this book you are invited to go down the historic farm's paths to see the quilt shaped gardens in bloom and discover how the farmstead buildings are used in the present time. You also will learn gardening secrets and tips about organic techniques. In addition, you will learn how to grow and use favorite culinary herbs.

You will enjoy scenes of Stream Cliff's Twigs and Sprigs Tearoom and also views of Stream Cliff Farm Winery. Herb and wine-enhanced recipes from some of the most requested dishes served at the farm are shared, as are recipes that have been demonstrated at the Farm's Cooking School. There are family secret recipes included. Be prepared to feel inspired about gardening, history and cooking from this delightful book.

Betty J. Manning

owner of
**Stream Cliff Herb Farm,
Tearoom & Winery.**

Acknowledgements

My thanks go to my devoted husband, Gerald, who for close to fifty years has been my anchor. Stream Cliff Farm was my dream, but the fruit of his labor made it much of what it is today. Thanks go to our children, Elizabeth and Greg, for their help in the business each day. Also, my appreciation goes to my wonderful staff who help make the dream a daily reality. My thanks also goes to my six grandchildren for giving me a song in my heart daily. I also am grateful to my daughter-in-law, Lauren, for her help with the book. A special thanks to my late, loving parents. They were affectionately called Poppy John and Grandma Dinky by some of the great-grandchildren.

Appreciation is given to Sondra (Knoy) Dunn for her assistance and also to April Yingling for her creative design work in pulling the book together. Thanks are given to editors Jennifer Jenkins and Suzanne Nevins and to publisher Linda Hawkins for their expertise. You have all been there when I needed you.

Dedication

This book is dedicated to my grandmother, *Luella.* She lived on this farm for many, many years and passed away when I was a small child. Those who remember her say I resemble her greatly. She was a woman ahead of her time and an accomplished organist, quilter and cook. She kept her spirit even though she lost four children and was widowed at a young age. My grandma persevered to keep the farm, and she loved it as much as I do today.

Index

Acknowledgements 4

Dedication 5

Introduction 8

Betty's Generation on the Farm 12

Secrets of the Gardens at Stream Cliff Farm 16

    Crucifix Garden 16

    Blue Bird Arbor Trail 20

    Dresden Plate Quilt Shaped Garden 22

    Grandmother's Fan Quilt Shaped Garden . . . 26

    Log Cabin Garden 30

    Log Cabin Quilt Shaped Garden 32

    Nine Patch Quilt Shaped Herb Garden 33

    Outdoor Sanctuary Garden 35

    Bridal Garden 37

The Secrets of Starting a Garden 38

Beautiful Garden Flowers 40

Herbs 53

Betty Manning, the Primitive Artist 62

Christmas at Stream Cliff Farm 63

Grandmother's Keeping Room & Learning Center 68

Aunt Betty's Cabin 70

Summer Kitchen Art Studio 71

Country Store 72

Old Historic Barn 74

Farm Animals 75

Stream Cliff Farms' Twigs and Sprigs Tearoom 76

The Winery 78

Recipes 81

    Secrets of Good Food 82

    Appetizers, Breads, and Salads 83

    Main Dishes, Vegetables, & Meat 93

    Desserts 110

This scene of our creek and cliff at our farm is where *Stream Cliff Farm* got it's name. The creek is beautiful in the spring when the bluebells and redbuds bloom.

Introduction

Welcome to Stream Cliff Farm! Come through the gate to this historic family farm tucked away in the hilly area of Southern Indiana. The farm is situated on an 80-foot cliff overlooking the beautiful Graham Creek, where clear water flows over wonderful limestone. Stream Cliff Farm, also known as Stream Cliff Herb Farm, is a garden business that sells a huge selection of herbs, perennials and annual flowers. It is also the location of Twigs & Sprigs Tearoom and Stream Cliff Farm Winery. The winery features about twenty hand-crafted wines ranging from the bold reds to lovely sweet, fruit wines. All palates are bound to find a wine to please. The Tearoom offers a wonderful selection of herbal foods and desserts.

Not only a thriving business, Stream Cliff is also home to the Manning family. The farm is now being enjoyed by the seventh generation with

six generations over the years living in the brick house. The great-great grandparents lived in a log house on the lower part of the farm. The brick home, circa 1836, was built by James Harmon, a bachelor from Maine. James Harmon came to Indiana in the early 1820's to collect his father's land grant for serving in the Revolutionary War. James Harmon's father served under Benedict Arnold. At the close of the Revolutionary War, General George Washington gave the Revolutionary soldiers land in the west, and his father's land was in Indiana. Even though Harmon's father was never able to come to Indiana, his son was able to settle on the land grant acreage. It took him seven years to bake the bricks to build the house. While building the home he lived in a hollow sycamore log and had pigs underneath the tree floor to help keep him warm in the winter. In addition to the brick house nd large barn, many of the buildings are original the farm. The Keeping Room that is used as a onference or classroom was originally built by the ailroad in 1868. It served as a boarding house for the men as they built stone fills for the railroad onstruction. When used as a boarding house, it eatured a large sleeping area on the second floor nd living space on the first floor. When no longer eeded as a boarding house, the farm used the uilding to store grain.

Other original buildings include what is lled Aunt Betty's Cabin, now a quaint shop the farm. It originally was my grandfather's acksmith shop. Another old building used as a shop is e Summer Kitchen. It is a sweet, small building near the randmother's Fan quilt shaped garden. The farm's main ft shop, the Country Store, was once a stable, and two

General John Hunt Morgan

other animal barns are original. Also on the premises are the remains of an old spring house that hopefully will be restored one day.

Mr. Harmon was the farm's occupant when the Morgan's Raiders came through this part of Indiana on July 11th, 1863. At this farm they stole horses from the cave in the side of the cliff. The Morgan's Raid is considered by many historians to be the largest event occurring in the North during the Civil War. In October 1863, James Harmon died and is buried near his farm. Being a devoted Methodist, he left his farm and reportedly $8,000 to the Methodist church. After a few years my grandmother's family purchased the farm from the church.

Gerald and I moved to Stream Cliff shortly after our marriage in 1965. Always loving old things, we became involved in making many old-time style, hand-crafted items. Gerald found my grandfather's old forge and made ornamental ironwork. I made cornhusk dolls and eventually made many dried flower arrangements. The need was so great for flowers to dry that more and more herbs and everlasting flowers were grown. Extra plants were for sale when we had open house during the weekends at the farm. Classes on crafting and gardening were offered,

and I would cook for guests using my precious culinar herbs. Finally, I decided to open a tearoom at the herb far for guests to enjoy.

My grandmother, Luella, lived more than fift years at the family farm. Gerald put in the many qui shaped gardens with the colonial style brick paths as tribute to her. The gardens feature several quilt design: Dresden Plate, Grandmother's Fan, as well as a garden the Log Cabin pattern. Also there are gardens with Hea in a Square, Crucifix Garden, and Nine-Patch pattern he Fairy Garden offers a playhouse for children, nd the Bridal Garden includes a wooden bridge. A ore recent addition is the Sanctuary Garden, a small utdoor church.

Eventually, our children joined us in working at tream Cliff Farm. Daughter, Elizabeth, a former high chool art teacher, is in charge of the Twigs and Sprigs earoom. It is often remarked that her art background apparent and affects the beautiful presentation of dible flowers on food. Son, Gregory, is a horticulturist nd is the farm's plant expert. He helps guests with all

matters related to gardening. Greg also helps Gerald make wine.

Today the farm retains the original acreage, as well as additional purchased land. Most of the farm is planted in corn, soybeans, hay and woodlands. The Winery began in 2006, as it served a natural fit for the family's interest in good food, gardening, history and art.

When my husband and I moved here, the home needed a lot of love. I began with a Victorian style; however, my taste in decorating has changed over the years. Today, the home is decorated with a much more primitive look than when we first moved to the farm. I use the term "country colonial" to describe my taste. I feature some primitive pieces with more formal accents. As a folk artist, my paintings are at home in the old house.

11

Generations of Our Farm Home

Betty and Gerald Manning

Greg and Lauren Manning

The brick farm home, circa 1836, has been home to six generations of family. The first generation of family (my great-great grandparents) did not live in the brick home but settled on another part of the farm in a log house that is no longer standing. The location is now home to son, Greg, his wife, Lauren, and their children.

When I was a child I always would say "Someday I want to live in Grandma and Grandpa's house." My parents had built a new house nearby. As a youngster, I would help my Daddy with farming, as I had no brothers. My jobs were raking hay, plowing and using the disc. The more complicated jobs like planting and baling hay were left to my dad.

The 1836 farmhouse took James Harmon seven years to build. The bricks were made from the red clay soil surrounding the house and were baked on the property.

After Harmon's passing in 1863 and shortly after the Civil War, the brick farmhouse has been home to six generations of our family. The picture above was taken in the early 1900's.

How could such

sweet and *wholesome* hours

be reckoned but with

herbs and *flowers?*

~ Andrew Marvel
(1621-1678)

Sweet Basil

Magellan Coral Zinnia

Anise Hyssop

Secrets of the Garden Path with Recipes

from Stream Cliff Herb Farm, Tearoom & Winery

owner *Betty J. Manning*

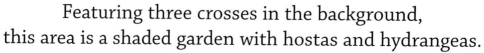

Crucifix Garden

Featuring three crosses in the background,
this area is a shaded garden with hostas and hydrangeas.

The Heart in a Square quilt pattern may be enjoyed in the *Crucifix Garden.* St. Fiacre, Patron Saint of the Garden, who represents blessing and protection, stands near the lamb statue.

GARDEN

Rustic Entrance

Continuing down the path of the *Crucifix Garden,*
clusters of impatiens and Dragon Wing begonias
overflow and hug the walkway.

Entrance to the

Blue Bird Arbor Trail

Blue Bird Arbor Trail

Dresden Plate Quilt Shaped Garden
A pergola frames the entrance.

 22

Hanging pink begonias bring color and interest to this garden.

$\mathcal{S}$tately urns filled with Coral Swirl impatiens mark one entrance to

Dresden Plate Garden.

*T*owering white pines offer shade not only to the strolling visitor but also to the shade-loving flowers.

$\mathscr{A}$ tranquil, romantic spot for tea nestled among nature's finest colors!

$\mathscr{P}$ink Baby Wing begonias and trailing $\mathscr{S}$ilver Falls dichondra surround an Alberta spruce, flowing from a mammoth urn in the

Grandmother's Fan Garden.

Alliums in bloom, surrounded by boxwood shrubbery
in this rock-walled garden.

Log Cabin Quilt Shaped Garden

Isaac & Lamb statue stand above a waterpool, accentuating this timeless garden made up of many perennials, including a variety of roses.

$\mathcal{L}$amb's ear and catmint frame the pathway leading
to the Log Cabin Garden.

$\mathcal{A}$ handmade twig arbor with clematis provides a seat to reflect on the sights of the

$\mathcal{L}og\ \mathcal{C}abin\ \mathcal{Q}uilt\ \mathcal{S}haped\ \mathcal{G}arden$

Nine Patch Quilt Shaped Herb Garden

basils, scented geranuims, and catnip are only a few of the herbs that grow here.

 Border and pathway leading to the Sanctuary Garden.

Outdoor Sanctuary Garden

*God grant me the serenity to accept the things I cannot change,
the courage to change the things I can and
the wisdom to know the difference.*
~Reinholder Niebuhr

Standing majestically over the white-picket fence, its petal edges appear as if fairies have trimmed them with pinking shears!

 Old-Fashioned Red Rose (Grootendorst)

Bridal Garden

Central to this bog garden is a primitive, wooden bridge that has been the site for many weddings. Countless frogs and water plants fill this lush garden that has as its seemingly natural cornerstones statues of the four seasons.

View of the Bridal Garden from the bridge with brick home in background.

The Secrets of Starting a Garden

1 Soil testing is useful when beginning a garden, particularly when considering amendments to improve your soil.

2 Determine whether plants prefer shade or sun in the choice of the garden site. Remove all grass or weeds then amend the soil. A small garden rotary tiller is useful to mix the additives with the existing soil. Soil additions often used include compost, perlite, lime, peat and sand.

3 If growing an organic garden, good choices to enrich your soil are compost, fish emulsion, kelp and worm castings. We use beneficial insects in our greenhouses, and they work wonderfully. If not growing organically, the slow-release fertilizer is easy to use.

4 In general, when beginning a garden, it is best to have a defined area and something to provide an edge to the bed. Some edging materials often used are bricks, stones, landscape timber or fencing. When no borders are defined, often the grass has a way of coming back into the beds.

At Stream Cliff, both brick and landscape timber have been used as edging. Another consideration is what to use to make your paths. At Stream Cliff, most of the paths are done in the colonial way, using bricks set in sand. Some gardeners prefer paths of gravel, brick, grass or stepping stones.

5 Herbs grow best in full sun or at least five six hours daily.

6 It is helpful when planting a garden, to draw a plan on paper with a plant list. As a rule, most plants look best when planted in odd numbers such as three or five of a kind. At bloom time, a real impact is made.

7 Consider putting tall plants in the back, medium plants in the center and low growing plants along the borders for a lush appearance.

8 I like a centerpiece in a garden. A statue, bee skep or decorative urn are nice choices.

Methods of Propagating Plants

Propagating plants is done in several ways. The choice is often determined by how easily the seed germinates and the patience of the grower.

Starting From Seed

For starting seeds indoors, sow the seeds in a sterile seeding soil, cover slightly and mist. Start seeds about four to six weeks before the last frost date in your area. Place the pot in a sunny spot or you may want to invest in an electric propagation mat and lights to improve the germination rate. Always be sure the soil is moist while the seeds are germinating. Some seeds have a very hard shell and require nicking the surface with a sharp object (called scarification) then soaking in water overnight. A few plants even require a cold exposure (stratify) to produce germination. (Larkspur seed is a good example of this kind of plant. Sow it in the fall and it germinates the next season.) When sowing seeds in the garden, always wait until the last frost and the ground has warmed.

Albert Einstein said, *"There are two ways to live: you can live as if nothing is a miracle; you can live as if everything is a miracle."* A germinating seed is a miracle! It knows the color it will be, the height, sun or shade preference and temperature requirement. I do not know how a person can be a gardener and not believe in miracles.

Taking Cuttings

Cuttings are generally taken from the tip of a plant. Place the end of the cutting in a rooting solution and put it in a sterile soil preparation. Roots form after two-to-six weeks for most plants, especially when cuttings are done in warm weather.

Root Division

I find root division is easy in the spring as plants emerge. Some people prefer dividing plants in the fall. A sharp spade is used to simply divide the plant into sections and then plant or share with friends.

Layering Technique

This is useful to do if you need a few extra plants. I find it works especially well on woody shrubs. Simply choose a low branch of the plant and scrape along the back side of the stem. Place it so the scraped area contacts moist soil. Put a rock or brick on the branch to secure it to the ground. In a couple of months when the roots have formed, cut the rooted branch off and you have a new plant.

Don't judge each day by the harvest you reap but by the seeds that you plant.
~ Robert Louis Stevenson

A person could live a very happy life if guided by this phrase.

White Oriental Lily
called **Casa Blanca,** this one is very fragrant and blooms in July.

**Stargazer
Oriental Lily**
is wonderfully fragrant.

Beautiful Garden Flowers

Geranium Container

The secret to great geraniums is to deadhead often, fertilize frequently and do not over water. They also like a weak epsom salt treatment every 2 weeks (1/2 teaspoon to 1 gallon of water).

Annabelle Hydrangea

These blooms are commonly used in large fresh flower arrangements.

Salvia, Indigo Spires
Rare, showy, tender perennial

43

Limelight Coleus
with Ivy trailing

Foxglove
Digitalis,
Camelot Rose

Nicotiana Sylvestris

Verbena, Lanai Peach
Sun, annual

Boltonia, Nana
A late blooming perennial

Coneflower, Echinacea Sundown
Sun perennial

Hydrangea, Glowing Embers
Shade perennial

Begonia, Dragon Wing
Wonderful shade annual

Hostas
Shade perennials

Clematis - John Warren
Sun perennial vine

Fuchsia, Gartenmeister
Sun annual

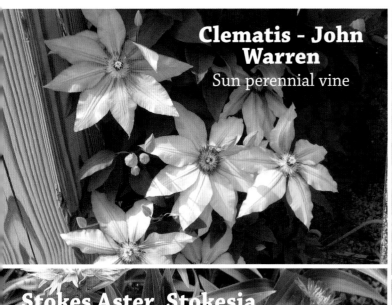

Stokes Aster, Stokesia laevis Klaus Jelitto
Border plant and sun perennial

Verbena, Lanai Bright Pink
Sun annual

Rodger's Flower
A tall part shade perennial

Dipladenia, Red Riding Hood
Sun annual vine

Tuberous Begonia, Rose Petticoat
Shade annual

Browallia, Marine Bells
Shade annual

Yellow Old Fashioned Iris
A bog plant, sun perennial

Asiatic, Yellow Lily
Sunray

Gaillardia, Goblin
Sun perennial

Nasturtium, Alaska
Sun annual

Roses
do comfort the *heart.*
~ *William Langham*
(1797-1856)

Knock Out Double Pink

Tihatian Sunset

Don Juan

Light My Fire

Roses, **rosa** Sun Perennials

Simplicity

Peppermint Splash

White Foxglove

Geranium Moss Basket

Torenia Basket

Coleus with Dragon Wing Begonia

ED's Vegetable Garden

Ed, our garden helper, grows vegetables for all to enjoy!

Can you find the frogs?

Little red wagons help guests carry plants easily.

*B*ack porch of our home
highlighting the path to the courtyard,
which borders a shady nook on the side.

Knock Out roses in front of a tobacco stick fence,
bloom all season at the entrance of the winery.

Gold Yarrows, Blue Larkspur
and Silver King Artemisia

Herbs

Favorite Culinary Herbs

Basil ~ *Ocimum basilicum*

Sweet Basil

There are many types of basil, but some are the super star. Sweet basil is our most useful for general cooking. It is use in many of the Tearoom dishes, some of these are the pest for gourmet sandwiches. We also use it in our pasta salad an in soup. Sweet basil and purple basil are snipped over fres green salads. In vinegars, the cinnamon basil adds a spic sweet taste and compliments other herbs that are used. Th cinnamon basil is the main reason our Tearoom Pasta Sala has such a special taste. Growing: sun annual that is usuall grown from seed.

Bay ~ *Laurus nobilis*

The leaf of this herb is delicious in soups, stews, marinades or any dish that is simmered for a long time. Remove the bay leaf before serving. Growing: hardy to about 15-20° F, will grow well in full sun or part sun. Leaves dry well.

Bay

Burnet, Salad ~ *Poterium sanguisorba*

The flavor is similar to cucumbers. It is nice to use in dips a it is easy to chop in a blender, or chop a few leaves to add t cream cheese for little tea sandwiches. Growing: this plant i a sun perennial. It stays more attractive if the seed heads ar removed.

Burnet

Chives ~ *Allium schoenoprasum*

When considering how to use chives, always think about a delicate onion flavor and you will not go wrong. Use in soups, cream cheese or snip over salads. The beautiful bloom is also edible and is lovely on plates or added to vinegars. Growing: sun-loving perennial that reseeds if blooms are not picked.

Chives

Cilantro/Coriander ~ *Coriandrum sativum*

Cilantro - Coriander plant is useful both as a fresh leaf (cilantro) or seed (coriander). Cilantro is a deliciously crisp flavor added to salsa and the seed (coriander) is delightful ground and used as a spice flavor for cookies, cakes and breads. Growing: annual; full sun, reseeding. Successive plantings about every month ensures a constant supply. Once the plant has dropped the seeds, the original plant dies but the seeds emerge to a plant the next season.

Cilantro

Dill ~ *Anethum graveolens*

This herb is one of our most frequently used herbs in the Tearoom. It is a dominant flavor in our chicken salad and also in the cheese soup. The leaves, known as dillweed, are the part most commonly used in salads, dips, butters and sauces. The seeds, which have a little more potent flavor, are especially useful for dill pickles. Growing: annual, full sun. For continuous production, successive planting, about once a month, is recommended. Dill reseeds freely if a few blooms are allowed to mature and drop seeds for the next year.

Dill

Garlic

Garlic ~ *Allium sativum*

Garlic imparts a lovely flavor to many dishes. One of our favorite ways to use garlic is in conjunction with rosemary. Sauté chicken in butter and olive oil with a little garlic and rosemary and it is just incredible. How delightful and creamy roasted garlic is on toasted bread! Or garlic mayonnaise (aioli) is wonderful on sandwiches. It has been noted for centuries that people who eat garlic seem happy; perhaps that really is true! Growing: this perennial bulb likes to grow in the full sun and is best planted in the fall, then harvested the following summer when the leaves die back. Pull the garlic, and either braid leaves or place with good air circulation to dry for best storage results.

Lavender ~ *Lavandula spp.*

Lavender has a pronounced floral flavor and is a lovely addition to many desserts. It is also useful with fruit salads, meringues and cookies as well as beverages. Generally the tiny flowers are removed from the stem and used as flavoring. Growing: this herb has specific preferences for growth. Full sun and well-drained soil with lime or gravel are basic requirements. Harvest when blossoms just begin to fully open. Grosso and Hidcote are two of our favorite cultivars.

Lavender

Lemon Balm ~ *Melissa officinalis*

Delicate lemon flavor, nice to mince for cookies, salad dressing, sauces and custards. Growing: easy to grow, sun perennial that reseeds often. Use fresh if available. This plant is also commonly known as lemon mint.

Lemon Balm

Lemon Grass ~ *Cymbopogon citratus*

This wonderful lemon herb is delicious with fish, in teas or with Asian cuisines. The inner stalk at the base has the most delicious flavor. Growing: this full sun, tender perennial is hardy to about 20-30° F. It grows nicely in pots.

Lemon Grass

Lemon Verbena

Lemon Verbena ~ *Aloysia triphylla*

This herb has the most lemon scent and is useful as a marinade for fish and chicken or may be used as an infusion for beverages. Growing: full sun, tender perennial that is hardy to about 20° F. Growth habit is that of a deciduous woody shrub. In our zone 5 climate, we put this plant in the greenhouse for the winter.

Lovage ~ *Levisticum officinale*

When deciding how to use lovage, a good rule of thumb is if celery is used then lovage is a great herb to use. It is often used in soups, sauces, or with meat dishes. Both leaves and stalk are delicious. Growing: this hardy herb likes full sun with rich soil. It grows quite large, growing up to 4 feet.

Lovage

Marjoram ~ Origanum majorana

This delicious tasting herb with its lovely fragrance i
used in the Tearoom as a dominant herb for ou
seafood salad. Often called sweet marjoram, as it is
sweet-smelling relative of oregano. Growing: sur
loving, tender perennial, hardy to about 20° F, so w
grow it as an annual in our zone 5 area.

Marjoram

Mint ~ Mentha spp.

A large family of plants with some of our favorites
being chocolate mint, a strong favored peppermint
with a dark stem. This one is used in our mint tea.
Another beautiful mint is the Kentucky Colonel

Kentucky Colonel Spearmint

spearmint, a Kentucky
Derby favorite for the mint
julep. The late Mary Peddie
was a friend of mine from
Kentucky. She said that she
was the person responsible
for selecting the name for
this wonderful spearmint. Another attractive mint, especially as
garnish, is the variegated leaf pineapple variety. Mints are great i
teas, in fruit salads, with chocolates, jellies, and of course, with laml
Growing: part sun, part shade perennial. One of the few herbs tha
actually likes damp areas to grow. Because it spreads so quickl
throughout a garden, I recommend growing it in a container, snippin
often and keeping it on a patio table. This herb is so wonderfu
everyone should have a pot of mint.

Pineapple Mint

Nasturtium ~ *Tropaeolum majus*

The edible blooms of nasturtiums are a main stay that we use as garnish for the plates in the Tearoom. The leaves are also flavorful as both the blossom and leaves have a wonderful peppery taste. Leaves may be snipped and mixed with fresh green salads, and the blossoms are delicious stuffed with a little herb cream cheese. Growing: annual, full sun. Picking frequently seems to encourage more blooms. Do not over fertilize as you will have more leaves than blooms.

Nasturtium

Oregano ~ *Origanum spp.*

Here at our farm we only use the white blooming Greek oregano for cooking as our experience has been that the purple blooming ones are inferior in flavor to the Greek oregano. This herb is so familiar in pizza, spaghetti, and tomato dishes, but it is also good with other foods like stews, fish and beans. Growing: full sun, hardy perennial, that may be used fresh or dried.

Oregano

Parsley ~ *Petroselinum crispum*

This herb is probably one of the most nutritious foods a person can eat. Varieties we grow are the flat-leaf, Italian parsley and the curly-leaf, Green River parsley. The preferred one is the Italian parsley. As a rule, we use parsley fresh in breads, salads and soups. The crisp taste adds so much flavor that it should be used often while cooking a wide range of foods. Growing: hardy sun-loving biennial. During the second year, it produces seed then it dies, so plant parsley every year.

Curly Parsley (French Parsley)

Rosemary

Rosemary ~ *Rosmarinus officinalis*

This herb is my #1 favorite herb for cooking. It is wonderful in ou[r] chicken salad or with cheese, beef, or pork. Rosemary is also nic[e] to chop and put in breads or even in sugar cookies. We do advis[e] adding herbs at the end of cooking, if possible, as it maintains th[e] most flavor. To use - and we only use it fresh - strip leaves fro[m] the stem and chop finely. If you must use dried, try grinding it t[o] make a powder. Growing: rosemary is generally hardy to about 2[0] F. There are a few cultivars that are a little more hardy such as Ar[p] but my favorite is still the old standby "officinalis." It loves fu[ll] sun and good drainage.

Sage ~ *Salvia officinalis* & cultivars

When thinking about sage, most of us think of Thanksgiving turkey and dressing, but this herb deserves a more broad use. It is wonderful in slaw and chopped apples, and it tastes heavenly with pork and also potatoes. There are many cultivars of salvia, but the officinalis, also called garden sage, is fantastic for cooking. Some salvias are grown for ornamental use and are not for cooking purposes. Growing: the garden sage is a woody shrub that likes full sun and is hardy. As the plant ages, it gets rather woody with only a few leaves, so it is best to replace your garden sage every few years.

Sage

Tarragon ~ *Artemisia dracunculus*

French tarragon has a delicate anise flavor; the plant is steri[le] and is only propagated by cutting or dividing. The one common[ly] known as Russian tarragon, grown from seeds, is virtual[ly] useless. French tarragon is often used in vinegars or with chicke[n] eggs or cheese dishes. Growing: sun perennial, try to plant th[em] so that it gets some shade in the hot afternoons.

French Tarragon

Thyme ~ *Thymus spp.*

[T]his versatile cooking herb may be used with many foods. Some of our favorite uses include [sa]uces for chicken, fish and pork. It is also useful with potatoes, roasted vegetables and cheeses. [A] favorite variety for cooking is the Golden Lemon thyme (T. x citriodorus). English and French [th]ymes are also excellent for seasoning foods. Growing: thyme is a sun-loving, hardy perennial [th]at enjoys good drainage.

Golden Lemon Thyme

Betty J. Manning, the Primitive Artist, farm scenes

Christmas at Stream Cliff Herb Farm

Living on an old family farm brings a joyous, magical feeling when the holiday time comes around. There is much preparation and planning. Usually there is a theme chosen for decorating, and of course, there is the planning for special meals and new recipes. Often thoughts go back to how Christmas was celebrated by the many generations of our family that have lived here on the farm. I'm sure it was very simple, but special in its own way. My grandmother, Luella, lived here on the farm for more than fifty years. She was known as an excellent cook, quilter, and gardener, but she was also an organist (using an old pump organ) for the church. It would be interesting to know the old Christmas carols Grandma would have played on the pump organ. She would have enjoyed all the excitement of today.

63

Our holiday time actually starts in early November as there are scheduled events for the herb farm, so decorating time comes early. In the early years of our business, no artificial decorations were used, and we used everything natural; however, fresh decorations needed to be changed several times to keep them attractive for the holidays. Eventually, practicality and improvement of more permanent decorations encouraged us to use them for part of the decorating. A friend, who was a floral designer, taught me to mix natural and artificial decorations together, as she said the eye always sees the natural thing. It is very true. So now we do this, which has created a lot less holiday stress. When Christmas approaches, of course, fresh greens and real floral arrangements are made for the holy celebration our family enjoys. When our children were young, we had many living nativities complete with a donkey and sheep in the barn, and now with the grandchildren, it is time for that to happen again. Cookies, hot chocolate, and caroling in the home complete the evening.

Historically, herbs have played a very essential role in Christmas celebrations, especially those that are considered manger herbs, of which there are many.

Basil is a manger herb. One type was often used by priests to dip in holy water and was sprinkled as a blessing, thus it is called "Holy Basil."

Lady's bedstraw is considered to be the hay that lined the blessed manger. This herb has a delicate golden bloom that was often scattered in fields to increase crop yields, and it was used as bedding in animal stalls to ward off disease.

Pennyroyal historically was used in vinegar to inhale for those feeling faint. Today pennyroyal is considered toxic.

Rosemary is considered by many to be the mo[st] blessed of all herbs. It is known as the herb of remembranc[e]. Legend is that Mary threw her cloak over the rosema[ry] bush, and it was made to bloom blue.

Thyme, of course, grew abundantly in Palestine. [It] is a symbol of bravery, which indeed Christ endured h[is] pain bravely.

The Christmas Rose, hellebore, sometimes bloom[s] white and is a sign of purity. In many parts of the wor[ld] it blooms around Christmas. In places like the Midwe[st] it blooms near Easter, and it is referred to as Lente[n] Rose.

As a child the most commo[n] treat I received was what I calle[d] "The Lurton Store Treat." It wa[s] given by teachers, bus driver[s] Sunday School teachers and anyo[ne] in the community that wanted [to] show children a little kindness. Th[e] treat consisted of a small brow[n] paper bag filled with an orange, a[n] apple, unshelled peanuts, chocolat[e] bonbons, and orange slice candie[s]. The bag was topped with a nic[e] candy cane and tied by a string jus[t] below the neck of the candy cane.

Lurton Store in Commiske[y] is about one mile from our farm, i[n] the rolling hills of Southern Indian[a] about eighteen miles northwest o[f] the Ohio River. It was a gatherin[g] place for all neighbors. My father said that in the 1920[s] Mr. Lurton bought candy by the boxcar load. Commiske[y] is a little community that began when the railroad wen[t] through in the 1870s. The story goes that Commiske[y] was supposed to be located a few miles north of th[e] current location, but when attempting to set off th[e] depot sign, the train could not stop where it was suppose[d] to, so it coasted downhill to a place where Commiskey i[s] oday. The depot was built where the sign was, and the illage grew around the depot. Prior to being called Commiskey, this area was once known as Hopewell. As a hild, we went there every Saturday night because they had a television. Most homes at that time did not have a elevision. I remember when my Grandpa George saw a owboy show for the first time, and someone was shot. He said, "They really didn't kill him, did they?" Lurton's vas a true place of community activity.

On our family farm we had many chickens, and I vas assigned to gather the eggs. We sold the largest eggs o the Eaton's Hatchery in North Vernon, and the regular ize eggs we took to Lurton's Store and traded for our groceries. I tell my children that this is the way trading vas done, and they think I grew up in the "Dark Ages!"

Actually, we were quite self-sufficient and bought only what we did not produce. My family always had our own beef, pork, poultry and eggs. The garden provided all our vegetables and salads. The orchard provided fruits, and the edge of fields were full of blackberries. My mom and grandmas were wonderful cooks, so food was in a great abundance, but canning for our family was a huge task. My sister, Nancy, and I laugh because when we were children, there were always pies, cookies and cakes. When Daddy developed diabetes, that all stopped and our meals were never the same! Daddy worked his entire life as a farmer and never worked even one day of his life for someone else. He and my mom had two girls. My older sister liked indoor chores, but I did not, so I would help Daddy with farming tasks. Maybe that is why I got

Most carved Santas were done by Betty

involved as a gardener. I would tell him growing plants was my way of farming, only I just farmed in pots; however, I do not think he ever considered that real farming!

Our community was blessed with a number of people that filled the role of aunts, uncles and grandparents even though they were not biologically related. Neighbors Grampy and Granny Abbott lived just over and through the field, and Grandpa George had a farm lane cut through the field to their home. We visited them often. Grampy had horses, and Granny was a wildflower lover, so I guess that is why I have enjoyed a lifelong passion for horses and wildflowers.

At Christmas, there were at least eight elderly ladies, plus Grampy, Mr. Mathesis (neighbor), and our relatives that were on my Christmas list to be remembered. One Christmas Eve, our family decided we would make up some of the Lurton Store treats of my childhood to take with the flannel gowns and shirts. The children decided someone should be Santa, and Elizabeth, our daughter, volunteered to be Santa. She was about sixteen years old at the time. The elderly folks thought it was wonderful that Santa was a girl that magical Christmas Eve.

In recent years, Christmas has changed. None on the list of aunts, uncles and precious elderly neighbors are around to deliver flannel

gowns or shirts to

on Christmas Eve. However, the magic of the wonderful Christmas celebration remains important to our family. The lovely small church where we attend has a beautiful candlelight communion. The main level of the church seats about forty and the balcony also seats about forty. Christmas carols are sung at the candlelight communion service. At the end of the service, all the lights are turned out, each person

Cloth Santa made by Bonnie Wells

holds a lighted candle and we sing Silent Night. The glow is so beautiful that one does not want to turn the lights on and disturb the moment.

For Thanksgiving, when our whole family gathers from many states, a delicious meal is enjoyed by all with ham and turkey and all the trimmings. But for Christmas, the immediate family requests beef tenderloin, mashed potatoes, chicken & noodles, several vegetables, especially gingered carrots, maple Brussels sprouts and corn pudding. I like broccoli salad and Waldorf salad, and Gerald wants an orange-lettuce salad. Greg and the grandchildren like cherry pie. Elizabeth enjoys butterscotch pie, and we have shrimp for daughter-in-law, Lauren. When I have a lot of energy, I also like to have fried biscuits with apple butter.

After our meal, the Christmas story is read, and carols are sung. We have a time that each child gives a gift of talent, either a reading, a song or some little performance. Pappy (Gerald) always has to go check the animals while he prepares to transform into Santa, and then Santa brings many, many gifts.

67

Grandmother's Keeping Room & Learning Center

This building is one of the older buildings found at our farm. It was built in the adjacent field by the railroad as a boarding house. The men lived in the building as they worked for the railroad in the stone quarries nearby. Originally, it had three small living spaces on the first floor and one large sleeping room upstairs. In 1904, my grandfather moved it to the present location with his mules, Pete and Belle. In the picture to the right, he is the one seated, being pulled by his mules.

The large pulley and rope that were used to move the building are in the attic. My grandfather used the building as a granary. We currently use the Keeping Room as a classroom and conference area for bus tour groups and lectures. Also, Elizabeth and I use it for cooking classes. Quilt, art and craft shows are held throughout the year in this building. The Keeping Room is decorated in a primitive style with open rafters and a wooden floor. The large porch is used as a place for the many make-and-take projects that are offered.

Views of Grandmother's Keeping
Room & Learning Center

Photo by: Hearne Photography

*B*uilt in 1868, it endures as a place to
learn and grow through
educational classes and
exhibitions of quilts
and crafts.

Grandmother's Keeping Room
A Nature and Traditional Craft Learning Center

Aunt Betty's Cabin

This building was once my grandfather's blacksmith shop. The porch, situated next to the greenhouse is convenient for plant sales. The natural wood structure of a traditional post-and-beam construction presents a warm welcome to visitors as they visit the gift shop in this building.

Summer Kitchen Art Studio

The Summer Kitchen was once used for food preparation and canning during the days when the kitchen stove was wood fueled. This was before the days of air conditioning, so it kept a lot of heat out of the home.

Originally at our farm, the Summer Kitchen was twice as long as the current building. It has been said that at one time Dr. Matthews, from Commiskey, used this building as his office. The Summer Kitchen is also used as a gift shop and sometimes doubles as an art studio.

Country Store

The Country Store at our farm was once used as a stable many, many years ago. The building has four small rooms of a rustic theme with gray barn board walls. It is the area that many gift and garden items are displayed and sold. This building is original to our farm.

*Winterberries Seem
to Glow at Sunset*

When James Harmon came to Indiana from Maine in the 1820s, he constructed the old barn before building the brick house. It has huge timbers, indicating the size of the trees at the time. Once an archeology professor remarked that the oldest trees on a farm are no doubt in its barn. The old barn has been home to hundreds of farm animals over the years. Today, painted quilt blocks hang on the barn as a tribute to the many quilters of the family.

Historic Old Barn

Stream Cliff Farm has animals that *delight* our vistors, the *young* and those *young at heart.*

Stream Cliff Farm's
Twigs and Sprigs Tearoom

Years ago in a magazine I read that **tea for a gardener is not a beverage but a lifestyle.** I do not know the author of the statement, but when I read it, I thought, **YES! That is so true.**

When you visit Stream Cliff Farm, you will find in the Tearoom a garden area that has larg windows overlooking the colorful array of plants with butterflies and hummingbirds galore. Th other room has a floral mural with six flower fairies representing each of our grandchildren. I painte most of the mural, but daughter, Elizabeth, painted the flower fairies and the tea scene. The mur covers two walls.

Each plate is garnished with edible flowers such as pansies, nasturtiums and rose petals (a pesticide free, and please note that not all flowers are edible). You will also find a garnish of a culinar herb alongside the colorful blossoms. Floral tablecloths and fresh flowers are on each table. Th Tearoom seats about seventy people inside and has seating for twenty on the porch.

Herbs are used in the food preparation and teas. The most popular menu items are Dil Rosemary Chicken Salad, Tearoom Pasta Salad and, of course, the homemade desserts. The mos popular are Blackberry Cobbler with Vanilla Ice Cream and Hummingbird Cake. There is a wid selection of gourmet sandwiches, salads, soups, desserts and beverages from which to choose, as we as our own wine which is made here on our farm. The food and drink of the Tearoom are exceptiona because they are personally prepared by us, using the freshest ingredients and herbs available.

The Tearoom, initially, was a greenhouse. I thought a glass roof was going to be wonderful for the herb enthusiast to enjoy a cup of tea and a delicate sandwich while shopping for plants. However, Indiana summers proved much too hot to use a plant conservatory as a tearoom, so the building had to be redesigned. The farm location is very rural, and I am sure when it was decided to put in a tearoom that neighbors must have thought it a strange idea. Even so, we are thankful that it has been and continues to be hugely successful, due much in part to daughter, Elizabeth, and her wonderful staff.

Elizabeth Manning

A heartfelt welcome woven into the entrance of the Tearoom.

Twigs & Sprigs

TWIGS & SPRIGS TEAROOM

Inside seating, abundant with natural lighting.

Tearoom mural, painted by Betty and Elizabeth

The Winery

The Winery is located in the building that was my husband Gerald's blacksmith shop. The tasting room is in what was originally the porch of the building and is decorated with red and white. This room has a cherry wood counter, made from local cherry trees, that is used for wine sampling. A horse theme is displayed on all wine labels, with one special exception: our Pink Pig wine (see insert below) features a label drawn by one of our granddaughters when she was but five years old. The back of this building is where the wine is made, stored, bottled and labeled.

Photo courtesy of Indiana Wine Grape Council/King Shots Photography

The style of wine we make was selected after much thought of our customers' preference. There are ine lovely dry wines. On the sweeter side there are about eleven wines from which to choose. Probably the umber-one seller is Grandpa's Blackberry wine. Many people tell us it is the best blackberry wine they have asted, and we tend to agree. A very popular black currant wine we offer is called Kentucky Stud, named after eneral John Hunt Morgan's steed. He rode his big, red stallion in one door and out the other of his Kentucky ome as a bold statement that he was beginning his Civil War raid. Since horse-themed labels are used on the ines, it seemed fitting to name one wine after this famous horse that General Morgan most probably rode o our farm on his historical raid in 1863.

Grow
where you are
planted.

~ Author Unknown

Recipes

Secrets of Good Food

1. Always use the freshest and purest ingredients available, an example of this is unsalted butter. It has a shorter shelf life than the salt preserved butter. Thus, the unsalted butter is fresher and purer in flavor. Try to avoid synthetic flavors as much as possible.

2. Keep good vanilla on hand and use it freely. Place 6-8 whole vanilla beans split lengthwise, in a bottle of brandy and infuse for a month. Replenish new vanilla beans as needed but don't throw away the old ones. Your vanilla will be delicious.

3. Put a small amount of nutmeg in food. Nutmeg has a subtle, but hidden flavor and is so delicious. To store a whole nutmeg, keep it in a sealed container, and grate it as needed.

4. Use fresh herbs when available; if using dried herbs reduce the amount by one half to one third. To give an herbal flavor by infusion or to make an herbal beverage (also known as a tisane) start by boiling a few cups of water. Remove from the heat and add a handful of culinary herbs, cover and steep for five minutes. If making a beverage from this infusion and you want it sweet, add sugar while the water is hot. Juices such as lemon and/or orange juice may be added to this tisane. This is especially nice for lemonade, using your favorite culinary lemon herb.

5. To freeze basil, it is best to make a pesto, cover it with a thin layer of olive oil to keep the pesto from turning dark. Pour the pesto into an ice cube tray; drop one of the cubes into soups or pasta dishes for an instant basil flavor. Pesto recipe is found with pesto bread in this book.

6. Add a nice red, dry wine (2-4 ounces) to any beef dish or tomato sauce. Add dry white wine to chicken, pork, or fish sauces.

7. Keep fresh lemons on hand; lemon juice adds freshness to many recipes. It also removes stains and food odors from your hands.

8. Rosemary is best used fresh; if you must use dried, pulverize it to a powder and sprinkle as desired for flavor. To flavor soup, tie a bundle of your favorite herbs with a butcher's string. Suggested herbs are: rosemary, thyme, parsley and bay leaf. This is called a "bouquet garni." When the soup is done, the bouquet is easily removed. When beginning to cook with herbs, less is best. Your family and friends may not appreciate the taste of herbs if they are overused.

9. It is not necessary to cook with expensive olive oil as heat affects the subtle nutty flavor. Keep a high quality olive oil for salad dressings and a less expensive one for cooking.

10. Pepper is full of antioxidants which improve one's health; use it generously, I prefer freshly ground.

11. Parsley is one of the most nutritious foods to be found, so use it fresh and frequently.

12. The French culinary term 'mirepoix' refers to sautéing chopped onions, carrots and celery. I recommend cooking these vegetables in olive oil and butter because adding the olive oil to butter reduces the risk of burning the butter. Using these vegetables in this way adds much flavor to soups, sauces and hot pasta dishes.

Fresh herbs are used in the recipes in this book unless otherwise noted.

Appetizers, Breads, & Salads

Cucumber, Cream Cheese Triangles

1 1/2 cups cream cheese, softened
3 tablespoons salad burnet leaves, chopped
2 tablespoons parsley, chopped
1 tablespoon onion, minced
1/2 cup cucumber, seeded, finely chopped and liquid removed
1 tablespoon celery, minced
2 tablespoons red peppers, minced
4-5 dozen triangles of bread (half white and half whole wheat, with crusts removed)

Mix cream cheese with all ingredients but bread. Spread thinly over bread triangles. Place a white piece of bread on top and a whole wheat slice on bottom. Garnish with a salad burnet leaf.

Asparagus Mini Wraps

2 packs asparagus (or about 2 dozen stalks)
8 strips cooked bacon or ham
1 teaspoon dillweed, finely chopped
1/2 cup butter, melted
4 tablespoons grated Parmesan cheese

Snap off the hard end of the asparagus and use the rest of the stalk. Boil in salted water until tender (about 4-5 minutes), place in ice water to set color. Drain well. Wrap 3 asparagus spears in a piece of cooked bacon or ham, secure with a tooth pick. Place in a greased baking dish, sprinkle with half of the butter and half of the cheese. Bake at 400° F for 5 minutes. Remove asparagus from the oven and put the dillweed in the remaining butter. Drizzle this mixture over the wraps and sprinkle it with the rest of the cheese.

Caramelized Walnuts

pound walnut halves
1/2 pound brown sugar, packed
1/2 cup butter
1/2 teaspoon cardamom, ground

Melt butter. Mix butter, brown sugar and cardamom together. Stir in walnut halves. Spread evenly on a baking sheet. Bake 10 minutes at 350° F, stir and bake another 5 minutes. Remove from oven and let cool 30 to 45 minutes before storing. Walnuts will caramelize when cooled.
Can be frozen for several months.

Cheddar Cheese Straws

1/3 pound cheddar cheese, grated
1 1/4 cups flour
tablespoons butter, cubed
1/4 teaspoon salt
1/8 teaspoon paprika
1/2 teaspoon marjoram, minced

Mix together, blend well. On a flour board roll out to 1/2 inch thickness. Cut into straw shapes about 3/4-inch wide and twist. Bake at 350° F for about 12 minutes until golden brown.

Dill Parmesan Crisps

6-oz. freshly grated Parmesan cheese
1 1/2 teaspoons garlic, minced
teaspoon dillweed, dried and chopped
teaspoon pepper

In a mixing bowl combine all ingredients. Press to flatten. Using a 2-inch cookie cutter, make approximately 18 circles. Place on a non-stick, ungreased pan. Bake at 350° F for about 10 minutes or until just golden in color. Cool before moving crisps to cooling rack. Repeat until all of the mixture has been used. Makes about 30 - 40 crisps.

Fresh Cilantro Salsa

5 large ripe tomatoes, peeled and diced
2 onions, finely chopped
1/4 cup hot peppers of your choice, finely chopped
1/3 cup cilantro, chopped
1 tablespoon lime juice
1/2 teaspoon garlic powder
1 tablespoon sugar
Salt to taste

In a bowl, add diced tomatoes, onions, peppers and cilantro. Squeeze lime juice over mixture. Sprinkle garlic powder and sugar. Salt to taste and mix well.

Basil Pesto

1 cup pine nuts, toasted
1 1/2 cups, basil leaves, packed
2 cloves garlic, sliced
1 1/2 tablespoons fresh lemon juice

1 1/2 teaspoons freshly ground
    black pepper
1 cup Parmesan cheese, grated
1 cup of olive oil

Place pine nuts, basil, garlic, lemon juice and 1/2 cup of olive oil in a food processor and grind as fine as possible. Add the salt and pepper. Slowly pour in the rest of the olive oil while the mixture is blending. Stir in the Parmesan cheese. To preserve the color use right away or cover with a layer of olive oil to store in refrigerator for up to a week. This may also be frozen in an ice cube tray and pop one out for soups and pasta as needed.

Pesto Buttery Yeast Bread

Use the following Buttery Yeast Roll recipe and instead of making individual rolls use the above Basil Pesto recipe. Roll out the dough, spread with pesto. Then roll up like a jelly roll. Cut into 1 1/2 inch slices then place on a greased baking sheet and allow to rise, bake at 350° F for about 25 minutes.

Buttery Yeast Rolls

packages dried yeast
/4 cup warm water
/2 cup sugar
1/2 teaspoons salt

2 eggs, beaten
1 cup slightly warm milk
6 tablespoons softened butter
1/4 cup vegetable oil
4 1/2 cups flour

n a small bowl mix yeast with warm water (under 110° F) and allow to bubble to proof" the yeast, which assures that the yeast is active. In a large bowl mix ggs, milk, sugar, salt and softened butter. Add yeast and oil then mix horoughly. Gradually add flour and beat vigorously until dough is very well ixed. Spray the top of the dough with cooking oil, cover with a damp towel and lace in a warm location (under 80° F). Let rise until dough doubles in size. unch down once and let it rise again. Turn out on a floured surface and knead r several minutes. Make 2 1/2 inch balls and place on a greased baking pan. et rise until double in size then bake at 350° F for 25-30 minutes or until golden rown.

ried biscuits can be made with this recipe. After turning out the dough on a oured surface and allowing it to rise, instead of making the 2 1/2 inch balls, ake smaller balls about the size of a quarter and drop into hot oil. Using a arge, deep skillet with a candy thermometer fill the skillet half full with egetable oil. Heat the oil to 375-400° F and carefully place the small dough alls in the hot oil. Do not put a large number of biscuits in the hot oil at one me or the temperature will be reduced. Fry until brown and turn over to brown oth sides. Immediately remove with a slotted spoon and roll in powdered ugar, if desired. Serve hot!

Guacamole Dip

8-oz. package cream cheese, softened
avocados, peeled, pitted and mashed
/4 cup finely chopped onions
/4 teaspoon garlic salt
/4 teaspoon hot pepper sauce
cup tomatoes, chopped
tablespoon lemon juice

1/2 teaspoon salt
1 teaspoon dillweed,
    finely chopped
1 tablespoon lemon juice
1/4 cup chopped cucumber,
    drained

ombine all ingredients, adding tomatoes last. Serve with corn chips.

Cinnamon Pecan Rolls

(Shortbread Style)

Crust
1 cup flour
1 1/2 teaspoons baking powder
1/8 teaspoon salt
1/4 cup butter
1/3 cup milk

Caramel Topping
1/2 cup brown sugar, firmly packed (divided in two - 1/4 cups)
1/2 cup chopped pecans (divided in two - 1/4 cups)
2 tablespoons milk
1 teaspoon ground cinnamon (divided in two 1/2 teaspoons)
1/4 cup butter, very soft

Preheat oven to 350° F.

Crust: **Combine flour, baking powder, and salt in large bowl. Stir well. Add butter and cut with pastry blender or rub in with your fingers, until mixture looks like fine granules. Add milk and stir with fork until a soft ball forms. Place dough on a floured surface and knead 10-12 times. Pat dough into a rectangle, refrigerate for 30 minutes.**

Topping: **Combine 1/4 cup brown sugar, 1/4 cup pecans, milk and 1/2 teaspoon cinnamon. Place in the bottom of a greased 9-inch round pan and spread evenly.**

Remove dough from refrigerator. Roll dough out on a lightly floured board to a 16x12-inch rectangle. Turn the long side to face you. Brush dough with soft butter. Mix the rest of the cinnamon with the remaining 1/4 cup brown sugar and 1/4 cup pecans; sprinkle over the butter.
Roll up the dough like you would a jelly roll. Cut the roll into 15 slices. Arrange the slices on top of the brown sugar mixture in the pan. Bake 20-25 minutes until slightly brown. Invert immediately onto serving plate.
Makes 15 rolls.

Cranberry-Orange Scones

/3 cup plain yogurt
large egg
cups flour
teaspoons baking powder
/2 teaspoon baking soda
/2 teaspoon salt

8 tablespoons cold unsalted butter, cut up
1 cup dried cranberries
1/2 cup sugar
1 teaspoon grated orange peel
1/4 teaspoon ground cardamom

Topping

tablespoon sugar
/4 teaspoon ground cardamom

1/2 teaspoon cinnamon

Heat oven to 375° F. Combine yogurt and egg and beat well with a fork. In large bowl, stir together flour, baking powder, baking soda, salt and ground cardamom. Add 8 tablespoons butter and cut in with a pastry blender or rub in with your fingers until the mixture looks like fine granules. Add cranberries, sugar and orange peel; toss lightly to distribute evenly. Add yogurt mixture. Stir with a fork until a soft dough forms.

Combine topping ingredients and set aside. Turn dough onto a lightly floured board and give 5 or 6 kneads, just until well mixed. Form dough into a ball; cut into 8 wedges. Form each wedge into a ball and place on an ungreased cookie sheet. Sprinkle dough with sugar topping. Bake 20-25 minutes or until lightly brown. Remove and let cool on a wire rack. Serves 8 large scones.

Civil War Cornmeal Cakes

cup stone ground cornmeal
/2 teaspoon salt
eggs beaten

1/2 teaspoon baking soda
1/4 cup buttermilk
2 tablespoons bacon drippings

Mix dry ingredients together and set aside. Combine buttermilk with beaten eggs. Then gradually stir in the dry ingredients and slowly mix in the bacon drippings. Using a hot cast iron griddle that has been lightly greased, put 2-3 tablespoons of batter. Turn once when the batter bubbles, serve with butter and syrup. In Civil War times these cakes were cooked on a hot "hoe" over a campfire, thus, they were sometimes called "hoecakes." Morgan's Raiders no doubt ate these on their famous Civil War raid to our farm during the Civil War.

Aunt Mildred's Zucchini Bread

3 1/2 cups flour
1 teaspoon cinnamon, ground
1/2 teaspoon nutmeg, grated
1/2 teaspoon allspice, ground
1 1/2 teaspoons salt
2 teaspoons baking soda
1 teaspoon baking powder

1 cup vegetable oil
2 cups zucchini, shredded
2/3 cup water
3 cups sugar
4 eggs
1 cup pecans, chopped

Combine dry ingredients and set aside. Mix oil, zucchini, water, sugar & eggs, then add dry ingredients. Mix well. Pour into greased loaf pans. Bake at 325º F 1 hour to 1 hour and 15 minutes. Makes 2 loaves.

Sage Fritters

24 large sage leaves
1 tablespoon butter
Olive oil for frying

2/3 cup milk
1 egg
1/2 cup flour

Using a deep skillet, fill half full with olive oil. Prepare the sage leaves by washing and blotting dry. Mix melted butter, flour, milk and egg then whisk until smooth. Heat the olive oil until almost smoking. Dip the sage leaves in the batter and fry, turning on both sides to brown evenly. Drain on a paper towel and serve at once.

Marjoram Seafood Salad

2 pounds crab meat mix
1/2 cup chopped red onion
2 stalks celery, chopped
1 green pepper, diced

1 tablespoon dry, cut marjoram
1 clove garlic, chopped
Sprinkle of black pepper
Mayonnaise to desired consistency

Shred crabmeat mix with hands. Add all ingredients except mayonnaise and stir Gradually add mayonnaise to the desired consistency.

Dill and Sour Cream Potato Salad

cups of new red potatoes, cubed, boiled and cooled
1/2 cups celery, chopped
2 cup red onion, chopped
cup sour cream
cup mayonnaise
teaspoon fresh rosemary, chopped
teaspoon celery seed
teaspoon dry mustard
teaspoon dried dillweed
4 teaspoon seasoned salt
tablespoons dill pickle juice

ut the potatoes into approximately 1-inch cubes. Boil until soft, drain, and cool.
hop the celery and red onion, add to cooled potatoes. In separate bowl mix the
emaining ingredients (sour cream, mayonnaise, rosemary, celery seed,
ustard, dillweed, seasoned salt and pickle juice). Pour enough dressing over
e potatoes, celery and onion to make salad creamy. Save any extra dressing for
delicious dip!
erves approximately 10.

Pumpkin Wine Bread

1/2 cups granulated sugar
1/2 cups brown sugar, packed
can pumpkin (15-oz.)
cup canola oil
eggs
3 cup Stream Cliff Farm
Winery's Sippin' Red Wine
(sweet)

3 1/2 cups all-purpose flour
1 1/2 teaspoons salt
2 teaspoons baking soda
2 teaspoons cinnamon, ground
1 teaspoon nutmeg, ground
1/2 teaspoon cloves, ground
2 teaspoons allspice, ground
1 cup chopped nuts
1 cup raisins

eat together sugars, oil, eggs, pumpkin and wine. Combine dry ingredients
nd add to egg mixture. Stir in nuts and raisins. Pour into 2 well-greased loaf
ans. Bake at 350° F for approximately one hour until toothpick comes out
lean. Let cool. Remove from pans and cool. Good to freeze ahead.

Tearoom Pasta Salad

1 broccoli head, chopped
1/2 cauliflower head, chopped
1/2 pound bacon, fried, drained and chopped
1/2 cup red onion, diced
1/2 cup frozen peas
1/4 cup raisins
2 tablespoons sunflower seeds
32-oz. box of tri-color rotini pasta

Dressing:
Mayonnaise to taste
3/4 cup red wine vinegar (We use our own herbal vinegar.)
1 1/2 cups sugar
2 tablespoons dried dillweed

Follow directions on box for cooking pasta. Drain and cool pasta with cold water. Stir together other ingredients. Stir dressing ingredients together separately. Mix pasta, vegetable mixture and dressing together. Chill 4 hours before serving.

Dill and Rosemary Chicken Salad

1/2 cup sliced small red grapes
1/2 cup diced dill pickles
1/3 cup sweet relish
1/3 cup diced red onion
1/2 cup diced celery
1 tablespoon finely chopped fresh rosemary
1 tablespoon dried dillweed
4 boneless, skinless chicken breasts
1 cup mayonnaise (I prefer Hellmann's original)
Salt and pepper to taste.

Boil chicken breasts and dice into 1/2-inch pieces. Stir together first seven ingredients until well mixed. Add chicken and mayonnaise, salt and pepper to taste and mix well. Serves 6.

Dill Slaw

1/2 pounds slaw mix (shredded cabbage and carrots)
1/2 red apples, finely diced
4 cup sugar
3 cup herb vinegar
8 cup lemon juice (plus separate tablespoon for apples)
cups mayonnaise
teaspoons celery seed
2 teaspoon Dijon mustard
4 teaspoon ground dried sage
tablespoon dried dillweed

Pour 1 tablespoon of lemon juice into 3 cups of water. Dice apples and store in lemon juice and water while cutting all three apples. Pour off all the water. Add the slaw mix to the apples. In a separate bowl add the remaining ingredients to make the dressing (sugar, herb vinegar, lemon juice, mayonnaise, celery seed, mustard, sage and dillweed). Pour enough dressing over the apples and slaw to make creamy but be careful not to pour too much. It will become more moist as it sets. You may prefer less mayonnaise. Serves approximately 8.

Pear and Gorgonzola Salad

ripe pears, peeled and sliced
2 cup crumbled Gorgonzola cheese
ed onion slices
reen leaf lettuce, torn
aby spinach

ressing:
8 cup olive oil
4 cup herbal vinegar
cup apricot preserves
alt and pepper to taste

Mix salad ingredients and put on a plate. Whisk the dressing ingredients together and pour over salad. Serves 6.

Spicy Apple Salad

1 3-oz. package cream cheese,
    softened
1/2 cup mayonnaise
1/3 cup sugar
2 tablespoons lemon juice
1/2 teaspoon cinnamon
1/4 teaspoon nutmeg
5 large red apples,
    cubed and unpeeled

1 8-oz. can pineapple tidbits,
    drained
1/2 cup seedless red grapes,
    cut in half
1/4 cup celery, chopped
1/3 cup pecans, chopped
2 tablespoons raisins
Lettuce leaf for plate

Mix cream cheese, mayonnaise, sugar, lemon juice, cinnamon and nutmeg together and set aside. Combine other ingredients except lettuce; add cream cheese mixture over apple mixture. Cover and chill. Serve on a lettuce lined plate. Serves 6.

Fresh Basil & Tomato Salad

5 large tomatoes, peeled, if desired
2 cucumbers
6 tablespoons crumbled feta cheese
12 ripe olives with pits removed
4 tablespoons olive oil
2 tablespoons balsamic vinegar
1 teaspoon salt
1/4 teaspoon freshly ground pepper
1/2 cup chopped fresh basil
1/4 cup Parmesan cheese

Slice tomatoes thinly. Score cucumbers lengthwise with a fork and then slice thinly.
Arrange tomatoes and cucumber slices attractively on a serving platter. Sprinkle feta cheese and olives on tomatoes and cucumbers slices. Combine olive oil, balsamic vinegar, salt and pepper with chopped basil. Pour over vegetables. Grate cheese over and garnish with a sprig of fresh basil. Serve chilled.

Hot German Potato Salad

pounds red potatoes, unpeeled
alted water
3 cup sliced green onions
2 cup sliced white onions
3 pound salami, diced
4 cup water
2 cup cider vinegar
1/2 tablespoons flour

1 tablespoon finely chopped dillweed
1/2 teaspoon rosemary, chopped
1/2 teaspoon parsley, chopped
4 tablespoons sugar
1 or 2 teaspoons salt or to taste
1/2 teaspoon pepper or to taste
2 tablespoons butter
2/3 cup sour cream

ook potatoes in salted water until fork tender, drain, and then slice potatoes as
ey cool. Sprinkle onions and herbs over sliced potatoes and set aside. In a
rge skillet, brown salami, drain and discard drippings. Add water, vinegar,
gar, salt, pepper and butter to skillet. Stir in flour and bring to a boil, then
hisk briskly. Remove from heat and add sour cream. Thoroughly mix potatoes,
nions and herbs.

Four Bean Salad with Marjoram

4 cup brown sugar, packed
2 cup cider vinegar
1/2 teaspoons salt
16-oz. can green beans, drained
16-oz. can kidney beans, drained
16-oz. can yellow wax beans, drained
16-oz. can butter beans, drained
3 cup onion, chopped
4 cup red pepper, chopped
tablespoon marjoram, chopped
teaspoon summer savory, chopped

a small bowl, mix brown sugar, vinegar and salt. Stir until sugar has
issolved. In a large bowl, add green beans, kidney beans, wax beans and
utter beans, pour the brown sugar and vinegar mixture over the beans. Stir in
ed onions, red pepper, marjoram and savory. Chill for 1 hour before serving.

Herbal Broccoli-Cauliflower Salad

12-oz. bacon, fried crisp and crumbled
2 1/2 cups broccoli florets
2 1/2 cups cauliflower florets
2/3 cups chopped red onions
2/3 cup pimento stuffed olives
5 hard boiled eggs, sliced

Combine salad ingredients, except hard boiled eggs, and mix well.

Dressing
2 3/4 cups mayonnaise
6 tablespoons sugar
4 tablespoons lemon juice
1 teaspoon salt
1 teaspoon pepper
1 tablespoon dried dillweed
1/2 teaspoon chopped thyme
1/2 teaspoon chopped mint

Mix dressing ingredients and pour over salad ingredients. Use only enough dressing to completely coat vegetables. Cover and refrigerate overnight. Top with hard boiled egg slices before serving.

Main Dishes, Vegetables, & Meat

Chicken Breast with Artichoke-Mushroom Wine Sauce

6 boneless, skinless chicken breasts
1/2 teaspoon paprika
Salt and pepper to taste
1/2 cup melted butter
2 tablespoons olive oil
1 14-oz. can artichoke hearts, drained
1/4 pound fresh mushrooms, sliced
2 tablespoons flour
2/3 cup chicken broth
1/2 cup dry white wine (Stream Cliff's Horsefeathers wine)
1 tablespoon fresh chopped rosemary

Sprinkle chicken with salt, pepper and paprika. Brown chicken in butter and olive oil over medium heat and transfer to 2-quart casserole dish. Save drippings in skillet for sauce. Arrange artichokes around chicken breasts. Sauté mushrooms in skillet with drippings for 4 to 5 minutes. Stir in flour and cook a few minutes. Gradually add chicken broth and wine, cook over medium heat stirring constantly, until mixture is thickened, and add rosemary. Pour over chicken and artichokes. Cover and bake at 375° F for 40 minutes or until done, no longer pink in the center. Serves 6.

Broccoli Gratin with Thyme

2 broccoli heads, cut in long spears
2 tablespoons butter
2 tablespoons flour
1/2 cup heavy whipping cream
1 teaspoon thyme, chopped
Salt and pepper to taste
1/2 cup grated Parmesan cheese

Boil broccoli in salt water until tender but still somewhat crisp. Melt butter in saucepan, add flour and blend with a wire whisk. Add whipping cream and stir vigorously. Add salt, pepper and thyme. Continue to stir until it begins to thicken. Remove from heat and add Parmesan cheese. Serve over broccoli. Serves 6.

Thyme Beef with Wine Sauce

pounds sirloin beef cut into 1/2 inch slices
4 cup butter
4 cup olive oil
our
alt and pepper to taste
cups Stream Cliff Farm Winery's Old Bo wine (dry red wine)
cup water
4 red onion, wedged
sprigs of fresh thyme

eat butter and olive oil in a large skillet. Coat each piece of meat in flour and
orinkle with salt and pepper. Add to hot skillet and brown on both sides.
ansfer to roasting pan and save drippings in the skillet for basting. Add the
ine and water to the meat (or roasting pan). Lay the thyme and onion pieces
ound meat. Cover pan and bake for 2 hours at 325° F or until tender,
ccasionally basting with drippings.

Stuffed Potatoes with Chives

large baking potatoes
-oz. cream cheese
tablespoons sour cream
tablespoons butter
4 -1/2 cup warm milk
tablespoons chives, chopped
tablespoons shredded cheddar cheese
4 -1/2 cup warm milk
alt and pepper

reheat oven to 350° F.
lace potatoes in salted water in a heavy pan. Bring to boil and cook until
otatoes are tender. Remove from water; let cool enough to handle. Using a
aring knife cut an oblong section off the top of the potato. Scoop out some of
he potato pulp as much as possible, being careful to leave the skin intact.
ransfer the pulp to a mixing bowl. Add cream cheese, sour cream, butter,
arm milk, chives, salt and pepper. Mix well with hand mixer. Stuff the potato
kins with mixture and arrange on baking dish. Top with cheddar cheese. Place
otatoes in the oven for 10 minutes or until reheated completely. Serves 6.

Apricot Stuffed Pork Loin with Thyme

1 1/2 cups dried apricots, finely chopped
1/2 cup pecans, chopped
1 small onion, chopped
2 stalks celery, chopped
1 clove garlic, minced
1/2 teaspoon salt
1/4 teaspoon pepper
1 tablespoon thyme
1 teaspoon sage
3 tablespoons molasses
1/4 cup olive oil
6-cups bread crumbs
1 large can chicken broth
8 pounds pork loin, double butterflied

Bring chicken broth to boil, add bread crumbs and stir to absorb broth. Cover and set aside. Combine first eleven ingredients in large bowl, mixing well. Add bread crumbs to apricot mixture, mixing well. Lay out pork loin: cover with plastic wrap and beat with mallet to flatten pork. Add salt and pepper to taste. Spread apricot stuffing mixture over the pork completely. Roll pork and stuffing like a jelly roll. Tie well with a butcher's string. Place in roasting pan with seam down. Bake at 325° F about three hours or until interior meat temperature reaches 165° F and meat is tender.

Honey Dijon Pork Sauce

1/2 cup butter
1 tablespoon Dijon mustard
1 1/2 tablespoons honey
1/2 cup meat drippings from roasting pan
1/2 teaspoon ground fennel
1/4 teaspoon ground cardamom

Melt butter in small saucepan: add mustard, honey, drippings, fennel and cardamom. Stir well and cook for 5 minutes while stirring often.
Slice Stuffed Pork Loin into 1 1/2-inch servings. Drizzle with sauce.

Scalloped Sage Pork Chops

-8 boneless pork chops (1-inch thick)
alt and pepper to taste
lour
/4 cup olive oil
/4 cup butter
/3 cup heavy cream
cup Stream Cliff Farm Winery's
    Golden Gallop wine (dry white wine)
/3 cup sour cream
/2 cup grated Monterey Jack cheese

2 green onions chopped
1 scant teaspoon rubbed
    sage, dried
1 teaspoon finely chopped
    fresh rosemary
1/2 teaspoon paprika
1 cup of sliced mushrooms

alt and pepper the pork chops, roll in flour and brown on both sides in a skillet
ontaining olive oil and butter. Spray baking dish with cooking spray and then
lace pork chops in baking dish. In the meat drippings, sauté the onions and
ushrooms with the rosemary, dried sage and paprika. Stir in heavy cream, wine
nd sour cream. Adjust seasonings then pour over pork chops and top with
heese. Bake at 350° F for 40 minutes or until pork chops are tender, no longer
ink in the center. Garnish with sprig of rosemary or sage.

Tarragon Chicken Breasts in Phyllo

cups mayonnaise
cup chopped green onions
/3 cup lemon juice
cloves garlic, minced
cups chicken breasts,
    cooked & diced

2 teaspoons dried tarragon
24 sheets of phyllo dough, thawed
1 1/3 cups butter, melted
1/2 cup freshly grated
Parmesan cheese
Salt and pepper to taste

reheat oven to 375° F. Grease 2 9x13" baking pans. In a bowl, mix mayonnaise
ith green onions, lemon juice and garlic. Add cooked chicken that has been
alted and peppered. Sprinkle chicken with tarragon and stir. Separate three
ayers of thawed phyllo, quickly brushing the top of each layer entirely with
elted butter and stacking on each other. Keep unused phyllo covered with a damp
loth towel. Place 1/8 of chicken filling in the center of phyllo stack. Fold the right
nd left side of phyllo inward to meet in the center. Fold top and bottom inward
verlapping. Place packet seam-side down into greased baking pan. Brush top with
utter and sprinkle with grated Parmesan cheese. Repeat process for the remaining
packets. Bake at 375° F for 20 minutes or until golden brown. Serves 8.

Beef Tenderloin with Rosemary Sauc

1 beef tenderloin (1/2 pound per serving)
Salt and pepper to taste
2/3 cup Stream Cliff Farm Winery's Iron Hand Wine (Cabernet Sauvignon)
1 bay leaf
1 clove garlic
1/2 teaspoon dry mustard
1 medium onion, chopped
1/4 cup butter

1 cup sliced mushrooms
2 teaspoons rosemary, chopped
1/4 cup olive oil

Salt and pepper the tenderloin generously. Sear the tenderloin in a hot skillet with a half stick of butter and 1/4 cup olive oil until all sides are brown. Place tenderloin in a roasting pan and bake uncovered at 425° F. Each time you chec the temperature, using a meat thermometer, place the probe in the thickest par of the meat. Bake until the internal temperature is rare, medium or well done according to your preference. For a 5 lb. tenderloin begin checking the thermometer at 40 minutes, then every 5-10 minute intervals. Allow tenderloin "rest" about ten minutes; the temperature will increase 10-15° F. Reserve meat dripping to use in sauce.

To make the sauce, combine wine, bay leaf, garlic, rosemary, and dry mustard and allow it to stand 15 minutes. Sauté the onions and mushrooms in the meat drippings, add wine mixture and cook until reduced by one-fourth. Remove bay leaf and adjust seasoning. Slice tenderloin and drizzle with sauce.

Homemade Noodles

2 cups flour
1 teaspoon salt
8 egg yolks
3 tablespoons half & half

1/4 cup butter (optional)
4 quarts of chicken stock
   with cooked chicken

In a large bowl place flour and salt together and mix well. In the center of the flour make a well (indentation). Thoroughly mix the egg yolks with the half & half and pour into the center of the well. Using your hands, incorporate egg yolk mixture with flour mixture using more cream if necessary. Divide dough into two balls, roll out on a floured board until thin (about 1/8 inch thickness), cut into strips and air dry for a few hours. Cook as described in following Chicken Stock recipe.

Homemade Chicken Stock (Broth) for Noodles

1 whole chicken	2 bay leaves
2 medium onions sliced	4 sprigs parsley
3 carrots, peeled, chopped	water
3 stalks celery, cut	Salt and pepper to taste

Cover chicken, vegetables, parsley and bay leaves with water and boil for about an hour, until chicken falls off the bones. Remove chicken from broth; discard vegetables, herbs, chicken skin and bones. Keep the quality meat as well as the broth. Salt and pepper the broth to taste. Before adding noodles bring the stock to a boil. Add noodles to the broth a few at a time, stirring frequently. Simmer until noodles are done, about 40 - 50 minutes; add the shredded chicken back to the broth. Check seasoning again and add 1/2 stick of butter if a richer flavor is desired.

Basil Spinach Casserole

6 slices of bacon, cooked until crisp - keep drippings
3 tablespoons minced onions
2 10-oz. packages of frozen chopped spinach, drained
1 egg
1/2 cup milk
1 teaspoon salt
2 teaspoons basil, chopped
1/2 cup bread crumbs
1/2 teaspoon paprika
1/2 cup cheddar cheese, shredded
3/4 cup Monterey Jack cheese, shredded

Sauté onions in a tablespoon of bacon drippings. In a large bowl beat egg and milk, adding salt. Stir in basil, drained spinach, crumbled bacon, bread crumbs, onion and 1/2 cup of cheddar cheese. Pour mixture into a greased 2-quart baking dish and sprinkle with Monterey Jack cheese and paprika. Bake for 30 minutes at 350º F.

Basil Chicken Rolls

1 teaspoon minced garlic
2/3 cup finely chopped mushrooms
1 cup Swiss cheese, grated
2 tablespoons finely chopped celery
2 tablespoons finely chopped onions
1/2 cup butter, melted
1/2 cup finely chopped basil
1/8 cup lemon juice
6 strips lean bacon
Salt and pepper to taste
3 whole chicken breasts, skinned, boned and pounded to 1/4-inch thickness

Sauté mushrooms, celery, and onions in 1/4 cup butter until just tender. Mix in chopped basil, grated Swiss cheese, lemon juice, salt and pepper. Divide the basil mixture among the flattened pieces of chicken. Roll each chicken breast and secure with a toothpick. Cover each roll with butter and place in a greased baking dish. Top with bacon and bake at 350° F until tender and juice run clear, about 50 minutes.

Baked Tarragon Wine Chicken

3 pounds frying chicken, cut up into pieces
3 beaten eggs
Salt and pepper to taste
1 1/2 cups flour
1 tablespoon finely chopped tarragon
1 cup bread crumbs (Panko)
2/3 cup grated Parmesan cheese
1 1/2 cups butter, melted
2/3 cup Stream Cliff Farm Winery's Horsefeathers wine (dry white wine)

Lightly salt and pepper each piece of chicken then dip each piece of chicken in flour that has tarragon added. Next, dip chicken in the beaten eggs that have also been seasoned with a little salt and pepper. Now coat the chicken in the bread crumbs that have been mixed with grated Parmesan cheese. In a roaster pan, place the melted butter and wine. Place chicken in the butter and wine, cover and bake at 400° F for about 45-50 minutes or until done and juices run clear, turning once to baste while baking.

Winter Beef Stew (Boeuf Bourguignon)

3 pounds boneless beef chuck roast, 1-inch cubes
1/3 cup flour
1/4 cup olive oil
1/4 cup butter
1 clove garlic
2 1/2 cups Stream Cliff Farm Winery's Old Bo red dry wine or Burgundy
1 1/2 cups water
1 teaspoon parsley
1/2 teaspoon dried thyme leaves
1 tablespoon rosemary, chopped
1 1/2 teaspoons salt
3 tablespoons tomato paste
20 small pearl onions
1 bay leaf
3 slices bacon, fried then diced
1/2 teaspoon ground pepper
2 cups sliced mushrooms

Roll beef cubes in the flour. Using a heavy deep skillet or Dutch oven, brown beef in the oil and butter, add garlic clove and cook one minute. Remove garlic and excessive oil. Add wine and water to cover the meat. Stir in herbs (or make a "bouquet garni") and salt. Cover and bake using Dutch oven at 325° F for 2 hours. Add bacon, tomato paste and onions to the beef mixture and bake another 40 minutes until beef cubes are tender. Stir in mushrooms and bake another 15 minutes. Remove bay leaf before serving. Nice to serve over noodles or boiled potatoes.

Reuben Sandwiches

2 slices rye bread
2 tablespoons Thousand Island dressing
2 slices Swiss cheese
1 16-oz. can sauerkraut, drained
1 pound thinly sliced corned beef
Butter

Spread 6 slices of bread with Thousand Island dressing. Top with Swiss cheese, sauerkraut, and corned beef and slice of bread.   Melt enough butter in skillet to coat both sides of sandwiches. Toast in skillet, until each side is golden brown. Makes 6 sandwiches.

Main Dishes, Vegetables, & Meat

Tomato Basil Pasta Cream Sauce

3 tablespoons extra virgin olive oil
4 tablespoons butter
2 cloves garlic, minced
5 fresh tomatoes, peeled and diced
2/3 cup Stream Cliff Farm Winery's Horsefeathers white wine
2/3 cup heavy cream
1/2 cup finely chopped basil
1/2 teaspoon nutmeg
Salt and pepper to taste
1 1/4 pounds grated Romano cheese, or your favorite cheese
1 pound favorite pasta cooked to package directions

In a large skillet, heat olive oil with butter. Add minced garlic, cook for a minute then add diced tomatoes and simmer until tomatoes soften. Add wine, cream, basil, nutmeg, salt and pepper. Simmer for 6-10 minutes, serve on a warmed plate over cooked pasta, add Romano cheese and garnish with a sprig of basil.

Baked Wine Chili

3 pounds ground beef,
    cooked & crumbled
2 tablespoons butter
2 tablespoons olive oil
3 medium onions, finely chopped
2 cloves garlic, minced
1 green bell pepper, chopped
2 teaspoons salt
1 teaspoon pepper
2 teaspoons cumin seeds, whole
2 tablespoons chili powder

2 10-oz. cans Rotel's diced tomatoes
    with chilies, original
2 15.5-oz. cans dark kidney beans
2 15.5-oz. cans refried beans
2 15.5-oz. cans chili beans
3 15.5-oz. cans diced tomatoes
2 cups Stream Cliff Farm's Running
    Horse Red wine
3 cups beef broth
1 tablespoon browning and
    seasoning sauce

In a large skillet, sauté the onions, garlic and bell pepper until onions are translucent. In a large roasting pan add all ingredients and mix well. Bake at 350° F for 1 1/2 hours, adding water as needed to keep ingredients under liquid while baking. More heat may be added using hot sauce if desired.

Dill Dip

cups sour cream
teaspoon seasoned salt
teaspoon salt
teaspoon onion flakes
tablespoon parsley
tablespoon dillweed
/2 teaspoon white pepper
/4 cup minced red peppers
/4 cup minced onion

lace sour cream in a bowl and add all other ingredients. Mix well. Cover and
efrigerate overnight. Nice to serve with vegetables, corn chips and chili.

Lovage Potato Cheese Soup

medium potatoes, peeled and diced
1/2 cups water
medium onion, finely chopped
/2 cup lovage, stems and leaves chopped
1/2 teaspoons salt
cups milk
/3 cup heavy cream
tablespoons flour
/4 teaspoon pepper
cup Swiss cheese, shredded
/3 cup sharp cheddar cheese, shredded
/4 cup butter
tablespoon parsley, chopped

lace diced potatoes, water, onion, lovage and salt in a large heavy saucepan.
ring to a boil and reduce heat. Simmer for about 15-20 minutes until potatoes
re tender. Using the back of a large spoon, mash potatoes, but keep the liquid.
tir flour and pepper into 1/4 cup of the milk only, then add to potatoes. Stir in
emaining milk, cream and butter. Cook until thickened being careful not to
corch. Add cheeses and parsley and stir well.

Cardamom Sweet Potatoes

3 cups sweet potatoes, cooked and mashed
1/2 cup milk
1 cup sugar
2 teaspoons vanilla
6 tablespoons melted butter
4 eggs
1/2 teaspoon cardamom
1 teaspoon cinnamon

Topping
1 cup coconut
6 tablespoons flour
1 cup brown sugar, packed
6 tablespoons melted butter
1 cup chopped nuts

Mix together first eight ingredients and pour into a 9-inch round casserole dish.
In a separate bowl, mix together coconut, flour, brown sugar, butter and nuts.
Sprinkle coconut mixture on top of sweet potato mixture. Cover completely.
Bake for 45 minutes at 350° F. This is a family recipe for sweet potatoes during
the holidays.

Marjoram Asparagus Casserole

5 potatoes
2 onions
1 teaspoon chopped marjoram
2 cups asparagus, (preferably fresh)
1/2 cup butter
Salt and pepper to taste
1 cup Greyeré cheese, grated

Peel and slice potatoes and onions, then place in 9-inch round casserole dish.
Add 1/4 cup of the butter, salt and pepper to potatoes and onions. Layer
asparagus and marjoram over top, then finish with remaining 1/4 cup butter,
salt and pepper over the asparagus. Add remaining butter, salt and pepper to
the asparagus. Cover well and bake at 350° F for 45-50 minutes until potatoes
are soft. Remove cover and spread grated cheese over top and bake for 5
minutes until the cheese melts.

Hot Penne Pasta with Herb-Wine Butter Sauce

16-oz box of pasta, cooked to package instructions
1/2 cup butter
1/4 cup olive oil
cloves minced garlic
medium red onions, sliced
cup sliced mushrooms
orange or red peppers cored and sliced
head broccoli, chopped
1/4 cup basil, chopped
teaspoon rosemary, chopped
1/3 cup heavy whipping cream
1/3 cup Stream Cliff Farm Winery's Horsefeathers wine (dry wine)
lb. chicken, cut into strips (optional)
Parmesan cheese to grate on top
Salt and pepper

In large skillet, sauté garlic, red onions, mushrooms, peppers and broccoli in butter and olive oil, stirring until vegetables are somewhat tender. After boiling pasta, add to sauté mixture and stir.

Sauté chicken in a skillet separately, then add to vegetables. In a separate saucepan, mix basil, rosemary, cream and Horsefeathers wine, heat for a few minutes to allow the herbs to flavor the cream and wine. Salt and pepper to taste. Pour over pasta mixture. Grate Parmesan cheese on top; add a sprig of basil for garnish.

Cilantro Mayonnaise for Sandwiches or Dip

3/4 cup mayonnaise
3/4 cup cilantro, loosely packed
tablespoon lime juice
teaspoon soy sauce
small clove garlic, chopped

Mix all ingredients in blender. Serve on sandwiches or as a dip. This is used on some sandwiches in the Tearoom.

Cardamom Wild Rice Pilaf

2/3 cup chopped and toasted pecans
1 2/3 cups wild rice
1 large chopped onion
1 teaspoon pepper
1 teaspoon salt
1/2 teaspoon ground cardamom
1/2 teaspoon allspice, ground

1/2 cup butter
5 1/2 cups chicken stock
3/4 cup chopped dried apricots
1/4 teaspoon nutmeg, ground
1/2 cup golden raisins
1/2 cup dried cranberries

Toast pecans at 375° F for about 6 minutes, then chop pecans and allow them to cool. Cook wild rice in chicken stock according to package directions (for about 45 minutes or until most of the liquid is absorbed, then set aside).

In a skillet, sauté the onions, then add pepper, salt, cardamom, allspice and nutmeg in butter. Add the fruit and nuts to the rice then mix well. Bake at 350° F in a greased 9x13" casserole pan, uncovered, for almost 20 minutes until well done.

Elizabeth's Baked Beans
(The best baked beans you have ever tasted!)

2 cans butter beans (15.5-oz.)
1 large bottle (1 gallon) of Great Northern canned beans
1 medium onion, chopped
1 pound brown sugar
1/2 teaspoon ground coriander
1 tablespoon smooth Dijon mustard
1 pound bacon, slightly cooked and chopped

Mix all ingredients in a large bowl. Pour into a large 9x13" greased casserole pan. Bake covered for 3 hours at 350° F. After 1 1/2 hours, uncover and stir.

Salmon-Dill Quiche

(See pie crust recipe in the dessert section)

-inch pie crust, baked
large eggs
tablespoons olive oil
tablespoon chopped fresh dillweed
tablespoons red onion, chopped
clove of garlic
/4 teaspoon salt
/4 teaspoon black pepper
cup half and half
/2 cup shredded Swiss cheese
/4 cup roasted red pepper slices
/2 cup shredded cheddar cheese
slices of tomato
-oz. baked or smoked salmon, chopped

Heat olive oil in skillet, then add onions and garlic. Sauté 5 minutes. Set aside. Whisk together half and half, Swiss cheese, cheddar cheese, eggs, dillweed, salt and pepper. Stir onions and garlic into cheese mixture, then add red peppers and salmon. Stir well. Pour into cooled, baked pie shell. Top with tomato slices, dipping the tomato under the liquid just enough to coat each slice. Bake on lowest oven rack at 400° F for 35-40 minutes or until set. This has been a "special" on occasion in the Tearoom.

Gingered Carrots

cups peeled baby carrots
tablespoons butter
/4 teaspoon salt
/3 cup Stream Cliff Farm Winery's Daisy's Delight Peach wine
/2 teaspoon finely grated ginger
/2 cup brown sugar, packed

Boil carrots in salted water until tender, then drain. In another pan combine butter, grated ginger, brown sugar, salt, and peach wine. Heat until butter has melted and brown sugar has dissolved. Pour wine mixture over cooked carrots, stir and heat on medium setting for 4-5 minutes, stirring frequently.

Fried Green Tomatoes with Basil

This is how Cousin Kathryn fixes these & they are delicious.
I added the basil.

6 green tomatoes
1 teaspoon salt
2 teaspoons minced fresh basil
1/2 teaspoon pepper
2 eggs, beaten
1 tablespoon water
2/3 cup crushed Ritz crackers
2/3 cup butter
1/3 cup olive oil

Choose tomatoes that are somewhat greenish-white just before they turn pink. Cut into 1/2 inch slices. Mix eggs with water to make an "egg wash." Separately mix salt, pepper, and basil into Ritz cracker crumbs on a plate. Dip tomato slices in egg wash, then coat slices in the seasoned cracker crumbs. In a large skillet, heat butter and olive oil until a drop of water sizzles when added. Fry tomatoes quickly, turning once until they are golden brown. Drain on paper towels. Continue adding coated slices, being careful to keep them separate, and keep proper amount of oil in skillet, while taking out finished ones. These are a delicious summer treat!

Shredded Brussels Sprouts with Chives

5 pints Brussels sprouts
1/2 pound bacon, cooked and crumbled
1/3 cup pine nuts, toasted
2 tablespoons chives, chopped
1/2 teaspoon cardamom, ground
Salt and pepper to taste
3 tablespoons butter

Remove cores from the Brussels sprouts. Place a part of the sprouts in a food processor and pulse a few times to resemble consistency of slaw. Process until all sprouts are prepared. In a skillet with butter, add all ingredients and cook for 5-8 minutes. Adjust seasoning.

Rosemary Roasted Potatoes

lbs. small red potatoes
cloves garlic, minced
tablespoon rosemary, finely chopped
tablespoons olive oil
teaspoon seasoned salt
/2 teaspoon cracked black pepper

Cut potatoes into 1 inch cubes. Place in a 9x13" casserole pan. Toss the potatoes with all the other ingredients. Bake for 18-20 minutes at 450° F until tender, stirring once while roasting.

Herbes de Provence Corn Pudding

/2 cup sugar
/4 cup cornstarch
 1/2 teaspoons seasoned salt
 tablespoon herbes de Provence
/2 teaspoon dry mustard
 12-oz. can whole kernel corn, drained
 17-oz. cans cream style corn
 eggs, slightly beaten
/4 cup finely chopped onion
/2 cup milk
/2 cup butter, melted

Herbes de Provence
The packaged blend we use contains a mixture of the following dried French herbs:
Rosemary, Basil, Thyme, Savory, Fennel and Lavender.

Mix sugar, cornstarch, seasoned salt, herbes de Provence, and dry mustard in medium bowl. Combine corn, eggs and onion in large bowl and mix well. Combine corn and sugar mixtures. Stir in milk and melted butter. Pour into greased 3-quart baking dish. Bake at 400° F for 1 hour. Stir once half way through baking time.
This recipe is one of our favorites for holiday time.

Main Dishes, Vegetables, & Meat

Desserts

Flaky Buttery Pie Crust

1/2 cups flour
 tablespoon sugar
'2 teaspoon salt
'2 cup butter, cubed
- 5 tablespoons ice water

sing a food processor add flour, cold butter, sugar and salt. Pulse a few times
ntil mixture resembles small peas. Add ice water a little at a time, pulse again
ntil pastry holds together. Form a flattened ball and cover with a plastic wrap.
efrigerate for at least 30 minutes. Roll out on a floured surface, press into a
-inch pie plate and flute the edges of the pastry.

Meringue

 egg whites
/2 teaspoon salt
 tablespoons sugar
 teaspoon cornstarch

eat egg whites, salt and cornstarch until mixture forms soft peaks. Add sugar a
ttle at a time, until egg white mixture forms stiff peaks. Spread on pie filling,
eing sure to seal meringue to crust on edges. Bake in a 425° F oven (watching
onstantly) until golden brown, which is about 5 minutes.

Desserts

Yummy Butterscotch Pie

5 tablespoons flour
1 3/4 cups brown sugar, packed
1/2 teaspoon salt
1 1/2 cups milk
4 1/2 teaspoons water
4 tablespoons butter, softened
1 1/2 teaspoons vanilla
2 egg yolks, beaten
1 9-inch baked pie shell

In top of a double-boiler pan, mix flour, brown sugar, salt, milk, water, and butter. Add beaten yolks while mixture is still cool. Place top of double-boiler over boiling water in lower pan. Stir constantly until mixture thickens and boils Remove from heat and stir in vanilla. Cover with plastic food wrap to prevent film from forming. Chill. Pour into baked pie shell. Add meringue to cooled pie.

Bourbon Chocolate Pecan Pie

1/4 cup butter, softened
1/2 cup brown sugar, packed
3 eggs, beaten
3/4 cup light corn syrup
1/4 teaspoon salt
1 1/2 cups semi-sweet chocolate morsels
1 cup chopped pecans
1/4 cup whole pecans
3 tablespoons bourbon
1 9-inch pie shell, unbaked

In a mixing bowl, combine butter, brown sugar and salt until fluffy. Then add beaten eggs, light corn syrup, vanilla, and bourbon. Stir in morsels and chopped pecans. Pour into an unbaked pie shell. Place the 1/4 cup whole pecans on top. Bake at 375 ° F for about 40 minutes until the middle is set. Serve with whipped cream or ice cream.

Gingersnap Banana Pie

Crust
1 1/2 cups gingersnap cookie crumbs
1/2 cup sugar
1/2 cup butter, melted

Filling
1 14-oz can sweetened condensed milk (do not use evaporated milk)
2 bananas, sliced

Topping
2 cups heavy whipping cream or 2 cups non-dairy whipped topping
1/2 cup powdered sugar
1 teaspoon vanilla

Crust
Grind 15-20 gingersnap cookies, enough to make 1 1/2 cups of crumbs, with the sugar in a food processor. Add melted butter and mix. Press into a 9-inch pie plate. Place in refrigerator.

Filling
Remove the label from the can of sweetened condensed milk. Fill a deep pan with water and place the unopened can in the bottom. Cover the can so the water level is 2-inches above the top of the can. Boil the unopened can for 3 hours maintaining a rolling boil. Watch closely to make sure there is always enough water to cover the can, as it could explode if top is not covered with water. Remove can from the pan and let cool for 15 minutes before opening. When opening the can, it will now be a toffee color. Spread into the pie crust. Allow to cool in refrigerator. Slice bananas over caramel layer.

Topping
If using heavy whipping cream, whip with a handmixer until soft peaks are formed. Slowly add powdered sugar and vanilla. Continue whipping until peaks become slightly firmer. Spoon whipped cream or non-dairy whipped topping over bananas. Refrigerate until ready to serve. Garnish with a beautiful edible flower, such as a pansy.

Delicious Peach Cobbler

2 double-crust pie crust recipes, one for top, one for bottom, unbaked
4 29-oz. cans Margaret Holmes O'sage Peaches Raggedy Ripe Freestone
1 15-oz. can apricot halves
4 cups sugar
1 1/2 cups cornstarch
1/2 teaspoon salt
pinch of nutmeg
1 cup butter, melted

Drain and reserve liquid from peaches and apricots. Mix the liquid with sugar, cornstarch, salt, nutmeg and butter. Cook in a saucepan until slightly thickened. Cut up peaches into smaller pieces add apricots and thickened juice mixture. Place bottom crust into a large chafing pan approximately 12"x18". Pour the fruit with the liquid over the crust. Place the other large crus over the fruit, slit a few places with a knife to allow steam to escape. Sprinkle top with coarse sugar. Bake at 425° F for 15 minutes. Reduce heat to 350° F for another 50 minutes.

Note: This is a large recipe and is great for potluck dinners.

Autumn Caramel Apple Pie

9-inch pie shell, unbaked
1 cup sugar
1/4 cup brown sugar, packed
4 tablespoons flour
1 1/2 cups whipping cream
1/2 teaspoon salt
1/2 teaspoon nutmeg, ground
1/4 teaspoon cardamom, ground
1 teaspoon cinnamon, ground
4 tablespoons butter, melted
5 large Granny Smith apples, peeled, cored & wedged

Combine sugars, flour, cream, salt and spices. Pour in melted butter. Stir apples into batter; pour entire mixture into prepared crust. Bake at 325° F for an hour and 15 minutes or until center is done.

Mama's Lemon Pie

1/2 cups sugar
2 teaspoon salt
1/2 cups water, divided
tablespoons butter
2 cup cornstarch
eggs, separated
4 cup lemon juice, fresh squeezed
tablespoons lemon zest
9-inch pie shell, baked

ix sugar, salt, 1 cup of water and butter in the top of a double-boiler pan.
eat until sugar has dissolved. Blend cornstarch with the 1/2 cup of *cold* water
nd slowly add to the hot sugar mixture, then cook over medium-high heat,
hile stirring, until boiling and clear (8-9 minutes). Using only the egg yolks,
eaten well, mix a little hot mixture into eggs and then slowly add eggs to sugar-
ornstarch mixture. Cook for 3-4 minutes stirring constantly. Stir in lemon juice
nd lemon zest, cook another 2 minutes and remove from heat. Put a layer of
ax paper on the top to prevent a film from forming. When cool, pour into the
aked pie shell. Cover filling with meringue and bake as directed in
eringue recipe.

Easy Blackberry Cobbler

quart blackberries, fresh or frozen
'2 cup water
cups sugar, separated
1/2 teaspoons lemon juice
'3 cup butter

1 cup flour
2 teaspoons baking powder
1/2 teaspoon salt
1 cup milk

a large saucepan place berries, water and one cup of sugar. Cook over
edium heat until sugar has dissolved, remove from the heat and stir in the
mon juice. In a 2-quart baking dish, melt butter. In a separate bowl, mix flour,
aking powder and 1 cup of sugar, then stir in milk. Pour this batter over the
elted butter. Spoon in berry mixture but do not stir. Bake at 350° F for 45
inutes. Batter will rise to top and form a crust as it bakes.

Chocolate Ganache

4 squares (1-oz. each) semi-sweet chocolate, melted
1 cup heavy whipping cream
1/2 teaspoon vanilla

Melt chocolate in a heavy saucepan over low heat, stirring frequently. In another pan, heat cream until hot but do not boil. Whisk the whipping cream and vanilla into the chocolate. Serve warm over cake or ice cream.

Chocolate-Mocha Cheesecake

Crust
1 1/2 cups ground chocolate sandwich cookies with white cream center
3 tablespoons sugar
4 tablespoons butter, melted

Filling
1 teaspoon instant coffee granules, dissolved in 1 tablespoon of water
4 8-oz. packages cream cheese, softened
1 1/2 cups sugar
2 teaspoons vanilla
1 cup cocoa
4 eggs

Topping
1 cup dairy sour cream
2 tablespoons sugar
1 teaspoon vanilla

Heat oven to 350° F. Combine cookie crumbs, sugar and butter. Press into bottom of 9-inch springform pan. Mix hot water with instant coffee. Combine softened cream cheese, 1 1/2 cups sugar, cocoa, coffee and vanilla, mixing well. Add eggs, one at a time, mixing well after each addition. Pour mixture over crust. Bake at 350° F for 45 minutes or until center has set. Remove from the oven; cool for 15 minutes. Combine sour cream, sugar and vanilla. Carefully spread over baked filling. Return to oven another 10 minutes. Loosen cake from pan; cool before removing rim of pan. Chill. Makes 10 to 12 servings. Chocolate Ganache (above) is nice with this.

Nancy's Praline Cheesecake

1/2 cups graham cracker crumbs
2 cup butter, melted
tablespoons sugar
8-oz. packages cream cheese, softened
1/2 cups brown sugar, packed
eggs, beaten
1/2 tablespoons flour
cup chopped pecans
tablespoons vanilla

opping
cup sour cream
tablespoons brown sugar, packed

lix graham cracker crumbs, melted butter and sugar. In a 9-inch springform
an, press crust into bottom. Combine softened cream cheese, vanilla, brown
ugar, eggs and flour. Mix thoroughly then stir in chopped pecans. Pour into
an over graham cracker crust. Bake at 350° F for 45 minutes or until center
as set. Remove from oven; let cool 15 minutes. For the topping, stir sour cream
nd brown sugar together. Carefully spread over baked filling and return to oven
or another 10 minutes. Loosen cake from pan; cool before removing rim of pan.
efrigerate for 5-6 hours before serving. Serve chilled.

Cream Cheese Icing

8-oz. packages cream cheese, softened
cup butter, softened
teaspoons vanilla
pounds powdered sugar
cup crushed pecans

lith hand mixer, combine cream cheese and butter, then gradually add
owdered sugar, blending until smooth after each addition. Add vanilla and
ecans. This is a good icing for many cakes.

Desserts

Hummingbird Cake

3 cups flour
2 cups sugar
1 teaspoon baking soda
2 teaspoons cinnamon
1/2 teaspoon nutmeg
1 teaspoon allspice
1 teaspoon salt
3 eggs, beaten
2 teaspoons vanilla
1 3/4 cups canola oil
8-oz. crushed pineapple with juice
1/2 cup applesauce
3 cups mashed, ripe bananas (the more ripe the better)
1 1/2 cups pecans, chopped
1 teaspoon salt

Sift together dry ingredients and set aside. In a large bowl, combine eggs, vanilla, oil, pineapple, applesauce and bananas. Gradually, hand mix in dry ingredients until well blended. Do not over beat. Stir in chopped pecans. Pour batter into three 8-inch round greased cake pans and bake at 350° F for 40-45 minutes until toothpick inserted into the middle of cake comes out clean. Frost the cake with *Cream Cheese Icing.*

Ma's Spiced Fresh Apple Cake

c. Sugar

cups flour
teaspoon baking soda
teaspoon baking powder
teaspoon salt
1/2 teaspoons cinnamon
2 teaspoon allspice
2 teaspoon nutmeg
4 teaspoon cloves
3 cup Stream Cliff Farm Winery's Captain Jack Apple wine

1 1/4 cups canola oil
2 eggs
3 cups tart apples, peeled and finely diced
(Granny Smith are good)
2/3 cup chopped pecans

Sift dry ingredients together and set aside. Mix wine, oil, and eggs; gradually add dry ingredients until combined. Stir in by hand the apples and pecans. Pour into a well-greased 9x13" baking pan. Bake at 350° F for about 45 minutes or until inserted toothpick in center comes out clean. *(Ma, Gerald's mother, didn't use wine; I added it.)*

Raspberry Chocolate Torte

1-oz. squares of semi-sweet baking chocolate
cup butter
4 cup plus 2 tablespoons flour
eggs, separated
2 cup sugar
cup raspberry preserves, seedless

In a heavy saucepan with low heat, melt the butter and chocolate, stirring frequently. Remove from the heat and whisk in the flour. Gradually add the egg yolks then set aside. With a hand mixer, beat egg whites until they are frothy. Stir in the sugar a little at a time. Beat until the egg whites are stiff peaks then fold them into the chocolate mixture. Pour into three 8-inch round pans that have been greased and floured. Bake at 350° F for 20-25 minutes until center is done and a toothpick inserted comes out clean. Cool before removing from the pan. Spread raspberry preserves between the layers and drizzle with the Chocolate Ganache recipe from this book. Delicious to serve with Stream Cliff Farm Winery's Pink Pig raspberry wine!

Coconut Cake

2 1/4 cups flour
4 teaspoons baking powder
1/2 cup canola oil
2 teaspoons vanilla

1 1/2 cups sugar
1 teaspoon salt
1 cup canned coconut milk
4 medium egg whites

With a hand mixer combine coconut milk, vanilla, sugar, canola oil and egg whites until mixed well. Sift dry ingredients together and gradually add to coconut milk mixture. Beat well. Grease two 9-inch cake pans and line with wa paper, then grease the paper. Pour batter into the pans and bake at 350° F about 20-30 minutes until toothpick inserted into center comes out clean. Cool on a rack before removing from the pans. Frost with *Mama's Never-Fail (7-Minute Icing* and sprinkle with coconut.

Mama's Never Fail (7-Minute) Icing

1 1/2 cups sugar
1/2 teaspoon cream of tartar
1/3 cup water
2 unbeaten egg whites
1 teaspoon vanilla
Dash salt

Put all ingredients except vanilla in the top of a double-boiler over boiling wate With a hand mixer, beat until stiff peaks form, about 7 minutes, keeping water a a boil in bottom pan. Remove from heat, add vanilla and mix well.

Cinnamon Basil Fruit with Lavender Cream

cups sliced fresh fruit (strawberries, kiwi, blueberries and peaches)
cups water
cups sugar
2 cup plus 1 tablespoon cinnamon basil leaves
1/2 teaspoons lemon juice

repare simple syrup by mixing sugar and water, then boil until sugar has issolved. Remove from heat. Add only 1/2 cup of cinnamon basil leaves, cover nd steep for 5 minutes. Strain off the cinnamon basil and discard, keeping yrup. Cool. Chop remaining 1 tablespoon cinnamon basil, mix with lemon juice en add to cooled syrup. Pour over fruit. Serve a dollop of *Lavender Cream* ver fruit.

avender Cream
2 cup milk
tablespoons honey
beaten egg yolks
tablespoons sugar
organic lavender flowers, or 1 heaping tablespoon of lavender
2 cup whipping cream

ook first five ingredients in a double-boiler for 5 minutes. Strain and remove owers. Continue to cook until thickened, stirring constantly. Cool with wax aper over top. Before serving, beat whipping cream and fold into cooled ixture.

Desserts

Chocolate Yule Log

Cake
5 eggs, separated
1/4 cup granulated sugar
1/4 cup powdered sugar
3 1-oz. squares of dark chocolate, melted

2 tablespoons self-rising flour, sifted
2 tablespoons cocoa powder, sifted
Chocolate shavings

White Chocolate Filling
2 1-oz. squares white chocolate
2/3 cup heavy whipping cream

Chocolate Icing
6 1-oz. squares dark
     chocolate, melted
2 tablespoons butter, melted

Preheat oven to 350° F. Place egg yolks and granulated sugar in a bowl and beat with a hand mixer on high until thick and pale. Stir in chocolate, flour and cocoa powder. Place egg whites in a clean bowl and beat until stiff peaks form. Fold egg whites into chocolate batter. Pour mixture into a greased and wax paper lined cookie sheet. Bake for 15 minutes or until firm. Turn cake onto a kitchen towel sprinkled with the 1/4 cup powdered sugar. Remove wax paper from cake bottom. Roll cake and towel up from the short end. Set aside to cool. To make filling, place white chocolate in a double-boiler, stir until smooth. Add whipping cream and stir until combined. Cover and chill until thickened and of a spreadable consistency. Unroll cake and remove towel. Spread with filling leaving a 1/2 inch border. Re-roll cake and place, seam-side down, onto a serving platter. To make icing, combine chocolate with butter and mix. Spread icing over roll. Using a fork, roughly texture the icing to resemble a log. Decorate with chocolate shavings and *Meringue Mushrooms.* **Serves 8.**

Meringue Mushrooms

2 cup powdered sugar
tablespoon cornstarch
2 cup egg whites
2 teaspoon cream of tartar
2 cup sugar, granulated

1/4 teaspoon salt
1 1/2 teaspoons cocoa, unsweetened
3 1-oz. squares semi-sweet chocolate
1 tablespoon butter

ix powdered sugar and cornstarch together. In a separate bowl and with a andmixer, beat room-temperature egg whites until foamy. Add cream of tartar, nd beat until soft peaks are formed. Slowly add powdered sugar-cornstarch ixture, granulated sugar and salt. Beat until stiff peaks are formed. Place in a astry bag fitted with a 1/2 inch plain tip. On parchment paper on a cookie sheet, ipe a 1"x1 1/2" stem. Then pipe a 1 1/2 inch cap, flattened with a moistened nger. Sift cocoa powder over caps. Bake at 200° F for 1 hour and 15 minutes. hut off oven and allow to cool inside. Remove meringues from oven. With finger, ake a small indentation under cap. Place a little melted chocolate in indentation nd put stem and cap together. Allow to cool. Place in airtight container. These re beautiful to garnish the *Chocolate Yule Log.* **Makes about 35-40 mushrooms.**

Louannah's Date Pudding

cup sugar
2 cup milk
cup flour
teaspoon baking powder

1/4 teaspoon salt
1 cup dates, chopped
1 cup black walnuts, chopped

a bowl, stir sugar, milk, flour, baking powder and salt together. Fold in dates nd walnuts. Pour into a buttered 2-quart baking dish.

opping: **Prepare 1 tablespoon butter, 2 cups hot water and 1 cup brown sugar, acked. Mix and pour over batter. Bake at 350° F for 25-30 minutes.** *Louannah as an elderly lady at our church and brought this to many dinners, she was kind o share this recipe.*

Pink Pig Raspberry Curd

1 10-oz. package frozen raspberries, thawed and undrained
1 cup powdered sugar
1/2 cup Stream Cliff Farm Winery's Pink Pig raspberry wine
2/3 cup butter
3 egg yolks, beaten

Using the thawed raspberries, with juice reserved, press through a fine strainer, keeping the pulp and reserved juice but discard the seeds. Put the raspberries (pulp & juice), powdered sugar, wine and butter in a saucepan. Bring to a boil, stirring constantly, then reduce the heat. Stir the egg yolks with just a little of the warm liquid then gradually add to the raspberry mixture. Cook for 4-5 minutes until mixture coats the back of the spoon. Cool. Wonderful over cake, ice cream or fruits.

Lemon Verbena Lemon Curd

1/2 cup butter
2 cups sugar
1/4 teaspoon salt
3 tablespoons lemon verbena leaves
2 1/2 tablespoons lemon zest
1 cup fresh squeezed lemon juice
4 large eggs

Using a heavy saucepan add butter, sugar, salt and lemon verbena leaves. Cook over medium-high heat until sugar has dissolved and the butter has melted. Add lemon zest and lemon juice and cook for about 3 minutes, stirring constantly. Remove lemon verbena leaves. In a separate bowl, beat eggs then put a little of the hot mixture into the eggs, stirring continually. Gradually add the eggs to the hot mixture and whisk briskly. Cook over medium-high heat, stirring constantly, until the mixture coats the back of the spoon which usually takes 15-18 minutes. Remove from heat, cool slightly, and cover the top with wax paper. Store in refrigerator. This is good to serve with scones or on cakes.

Cinnamon Twists

egg
/3 cup sugar
/2 cup butter
cups flour
tablespoons sugar
/2 teaspoon salt
1/2 teaspoons cinnamon
/2 teaspoon nutmeg

Beat egg with 2/3 cup sugar and salt. Add butter and flour and mix well. Knead until ball is formed. Roll to a rectangle about 1/2 inch thick. Mix sugar, cinnamon and nutmeg together. Sprinkle over rectangle. Cut into 1/2 wide strips and turn each to make a spiral. Bake at 350° F for 10-12 minutes until just golden brown.

Holiday Cranberry Wine Conserve

15-oz. package fresh cranberries, washed
1/2 cups Stream Cliff Farm Winery's Prancing Horse cranberry wine
tablespoons orange zest
/2 cup golden raisins
/4 cup sugar
naval orange, peeled and chopped
cup canned pineapple, crushed with juice
/3 cup walnuts, chopped

In a large saucepan, place cranberries, wine and zest. Bring to a boil and cook for 7-8 minutes until cranberries pop. Stir in sugar, pineapple, raisins, oranges and walnuts. Simmer for 15-18 minutes until mixture thickens. This is a lovely addition to a turkey and dressing meal.

Apricot Butter

cup butter, softened
/3 cup apricot preserves
/3 cup powdered sugar

Beat all ingredients together with a spoon, then refrigerate. Serve with scones or biscuits.

Ma's Powdered Sugar Cookies

1/2 cup butter, softened
1/2 cup sugar
1 egg
1/2 cup canola oil
1 teaspoon vanilla

1/2 cup powdered sugar
1/2 teaspoon baking soda
2 cups flour
1/2 teaspoon salt
1/2 teaspoon cream of tartar

Sift dry ingredients together and set aside. With hand mixer, cream butter and sugar. Add egg, oil and vanilla and mix well. Gradually, add the dry ingredients and mix well. Chill dough for at least one hour. Roll into 1 inch balls and place onto an ungreased cookie sheet. Then flatten with a fork that has been dipped in sugar. Bake at 350° F for 12 to 15 minutes or until light golden brown.

Hint: I like to bake cookies on parchment paper so they brown but do not burn.

Mama's Best Cookie

1 cup butter, softened
1 cup brown sugar, packed
1 cup granulated sugar
2 eggs
1 1/2 teaspoons vanilla

1 1/2 cups flour
1 teaspoon baking powder
1 teaspoon baking soda
2 cups quick-cooking oatmeal
1 cup shredded coconut
2 cups Rice Krispies cereal

With hand mixer, cream butter with both sugars until fluffy. Beat in eggs and vanilla. In a separate bowl, sift flour, baking powder, and baking soda. Gradually add to batter and mix well. Stir in, by hand, the oatmeal, coconut and Rice Krispies. Drop by teaspoonful onto an ungreased cookie sheet. Bake at 350° F for 10-12 minutes until just starting to brown.

My mother made these cookies often and had put the recipe in an old church cookbook. Carol, our farm "Cookie Diva," made and brought these cookies in one day, not saying anything about the recipe. When I tasted them I about fell over as hadn't had one for at least twenty years. They are still just as delicious as they were when I was a child!

Buttery Toffee Bars

cup brown sugar, packed
cup butter, softened
large egg yolks
cups flour
teaspoon salt
teaspoon ground cinnamon
'2 teaspoon ground cardamom
egg white, beaten
'2 cup chopped pecans
'3 cup English toffee bits

ream brown sugar and softened butter with hand mixer, then add egg yolks.
eat until fluffy. Sift flour, salt, cinnamon and cardamom together, then
radually add to batter and mix well. Stir in pecans and English toffee bits.
ith either greased hands or with wax paper, so dough does not stick to
ands, press into a 9x13" greased baking pan. Brush with egg white. Bake at
25° F for 12-14 minutes or until slightly brown. Cut into bars while warm.

Cousin Lida's Ranger Cookies

'4 cup butter, softened
'4 cup white sugar
cup brown sugar, packed
eggs
cups flour
teaspoon baking soda
'2 teaspoon baking powder
'2 teaspoon salt
cup rolled oats
teaspoon vanilla
'2 cup coconut

ream softened butter, sugar and brown sugar with hand mixer until fluffy. Add
ggs and vanilla mixing well. In separate bowl, combine dry ingredients, then
radually add to batter and blend well. Stir in coconut and oats. Drop by
aspoonful on ungreased cookie sheet. Bake at 350° F for 10-12 minutes.

Desserts

Mama's Peanut Butter Cookies

1/2 cup butter, softened
1/2 cup peanut butter
1/2 cup sugar
1/2 cup brown sugar, packed
1 egg

1/2 teaspoon vanilla
1 1/4 cups flour
3/4 teaspoon baking soda
1/4 teaspoon salt

Cream butter, peanut butter, sugar, brown sugar, egg and vanilla. In separate bowl, sift together dry ingredients, then gradually blend into the creamed mixture. Cover and chill for one hour. Then shape into 1-inch balls, place on ungreased cookie sheet 2-inches apart and flatten with a fork dipped in granulated sugar. Bake at 375° F for 10 -12 minutes. Makes: 4 dozen

Oatmeal Cookies

1 cup raisins
1 cup water
3/4 cup shortening
1 1/2 cups sugar
2 eggs
1 teaspoon vanilla
2 cups rolled oats

2 1/2 cups sifted flour
1/2 teaspoon baking powder
1 teaspoon baking soda
1 teaspoon salt
1 teaspoon cinnamon, ground
1/4 teaspoon cloves, ground
1/2 cup chopped nuts,
            pecans or walnuts

Simmer raisins and water in saucepan over low heat until raisins are plump. Drain raisin liquid into measuring cup. Add enough water to make ½ cup. Cream shortening, sugar, eggs, and vanilla with hand mixer. Stir in raisin liquid Sift together dry ingredients and stir in. Add rolled oats, raisins, and chopped nuts. Cover and chill dough. Drop by teaspoonful on ungreased baking sheet Bake 8-10 minutes at 375° F until lightly browned.
Makes 6-7 dozen.

Crème Brûlée

1/4 cups heavy cream
vanilla bean, split
large egg yolks, beaten
tablespoons powdered sugar, sifted
-5 tablespoons super fine sugar

ut cream and vanilla bean that has been sliced lengthwise in a saucepan over
edium heat. Heat until just hot, but not quite boiling. Set off heat, cover and
t stand for 12-15 minutes. Remove vanilla bean, scrape out seeds and put the
eeds back into the cream.

the top of a double-boiler, whisk together the egg yolks and cream. Stir in the
owdered sugar and cook, stirring constantly for 10 minutes, until mixture
ickens. Pour into individual ramekins. Place individual, cream-filled dishes in a
rge pan, with 1 inch water surrounding them. Bake at 300° F for almost 35
inutes until center is done, when inserted knife comes out clean. Allow to chill
r 8 hours or overnight, covered. Before serving sprinkle super fine sugar over
p about 1/8 inch thick. Place under broiler until sugar has caramelized and is
rown, or use a torch, taking care to not burn. Cool before serving. Makes 4
ervings.

Christmas Sugarplums

pounds mixed fruit (figs, dates, raisins and currants)
1/2 pounds walnuts
2 pound unsalted, shelled, pistachio nuts
2 pound crystallized ginger, finely minced
orange rinds from 2 whole oranges, grated
tablespoons brandy
ranulated sugar

a food processor finely chop and mix all ingredients except brandy and sugar.
dd 3 tablespoons of brandy to course mixture to allow it to stick together. Form
nall 1/2-inch balls, then roll in sugar. Store sugarplums in airtight container for
few days to allow flavors to mix. *This is a very old holiday recipe, modernized by*
e use of a food processor.

Nature's Splendor

"If the day and the night are such that you greet
them with joy, and life emits a fragrance like
flowers and sweet-scented herbs, is more elastic,
more starry, more immortal--that is your success."
~ Henry David Thoreau

"Though I do not believe that a plant will
spring up where no seed has been,
I have great faith in a seed.
Convince me that you have a seed there,
and I am prepared to expect wonders."
~ Henry David Thoreau

I have often thought that if heaven had given me choice of my position and calling, it should have been on a rich spot of earth, well watered, and near a good market for the productions of the garden. No occupation is so delightful to me as the culture of the earth, and no culture comparable to that of the garden. Such a variety of subjects, some one always coming to perfection, the failure of one thing repaired by the success of another, and instead of one harvest a continued one through the year. Under a total want of demand except for our family table, I am still devoted to the garden. But though an old man, I am but a young gardener.

"Just living is not enough,"
said the butterfly.
**"One must have sunshine,
freedom, and a little flower."**

~ Hans Christian Anderson
(1805-1875)

In this book it is my desire to give useful tips and inspiring ideas about gardening and cooking from years of personal experience. The book also represents the love and devotion a farmer's daughter has for her family and farm.

As an adult, now looking back to growing up in the country, it seems the soil of the farm of your childhood gets into your inner soul. Oh sure, you can cover it up with make-up and live in exciting, exotic places, but deep down the spirit of the farm and a simple life doesn't leave. It remains embedded to be passed on to other generations to love and cherish the land.

Making the world a more beautiful place is a goal we wish for every individual.

Gerald, my husband, and I have been blessed with a wonderful marriage, for this I am extremely grateful. We have worked as a team and are fortunate to have our children work with us daily. Our family has a dedication to our precious historic farm and have created a business with a mission of making the world a more beautiful place to live.